The
INTROVERT
who could

How to succeed in your career and life by nurturing who you are

ANDREEA SANDU

The Introvert Who Could
ISBN 978-1-912300-94-5
eISBN 978-1-912300-95-2

Published in 2022 by Right Book Press
Printed in the UK

A CIP record of this book is available from the British Library.

Contents

A letter from a fellow introvert

Hello, beautiful, introverted soul. I wrote *The Introvert Who Could* to help you change the way you think about being an introvert. It's the book that should have been written before those that teach you HOW – how to interact with people, lead a team, speak in public, socialise or meet new humans. I bet you already know how to do those things. But are you doing them?

I am and always have been an introvert. But I do crazy things like presentations, networking events or (covers her mouth in shock) coaching other people. It hasn't always been the case. Because, just like you, I read all the other 'how to' books but kept thinking to myself, 'But I'm an introvert.' Throughout this book, you'll not only get some practical advice for different situations, but you'll also learn to recognise the thoughts that you're thinking that are stopping you from applying that advice and how to change them.

Not everything you read will apply to you. That's OK. But there will be stories and journeys through my own thoughts that will leave you saying 'Wow, I feel the same'. Take what you need from those and let them change your life. Sometimes all you need is one single word to completely shift your perspective.

At the end of each chapter, you'll find a few 'thoughts to practise'. They're beliefs you can work on to develop the mindset needed to apply the practical advice. They usually make the difference between knowing how to do something and doing it. You can use them as daily affirmations, by setting reminders on your phone or sticking Post-it notes on your desk or simply repeating them in your mind in a situation when they would be useful.

Who's this book for?

As an introvert myself, I wrote from the brain and for the brain of an introvert. Whether you are an introvert, live or work with one, or resonate with any of the qualities of this personality type, you'll find some wisdom in the stories and advice I'll be sharing with you throughout the text. For me, an introvert is someone who:

→ recharges by spending time alone
→ spends a lot of time thinking and developing ideas in their mind
→ is a great planner
→ but prefers to listen rather than talk
→ and might struggle with being visible or sociable beyond a comfortable level.

The book is split into three separate parts, each solving one of the issues I see many of us struggling with: setting boundaries, feeling mentally and emotionally drained, and lack of social skills. Apart from making life a little bit easier, the work we'll do together will have a bonus side effect: you'll become a lot more productive. I believe that no matter what your goals are, you need time, energy and support to achieve them. By learning how to set loving boundaries and stick with them, you'll make a lot more space in your schedule for those activities that will make a difference and fill up your soul. By managing your mind and your feelings, you'll generate mental and emotional energy to flow through those activities. And by developing your social skills, you'll be able to ask for help and build a support team that's there for you whenever you need it.

I hope you'll be able to solve all the problems that are currently keeping you stuck, but before we really get started, I want to offer you one thought adjustment: being an introvert is not something that needs to be fixed. Yes, there might be some challenges, but your personality also comes with plenty of superpowers.

Introversion is not something that needs to be fixed

Until not too long ago, due to our society praising and encouraging extroverted energy and traits, I considered being an introvert a problem. I wasn't the kind who goes out to lunch with co-workers or spends too many weekends with friends. Social interactions were difficult, saying no was painful and spending too much time away from home was draining my energy.

I was that person who would rather live with a broken pipe than pick up the phone to call a plumber. And if someone called me, I stared at the phone until it would eventually stop ringing, so I could simply text back, 'I missed a call from you, was there anything urgent?'

In all my corporate jobs, when the time came for performance reviews, one single piece of feedback came up every time: I should speak up more, be louder in meetings, chat more. I spent ten years as an employee, and I heard the same thing over and over again, like a broken record. I was happy in my inner world, but the one outside thought I was fundamentally broken.

Then I decided to become an entrepreneur and found it even more difficult. Taking pictures, talking about myself, networking, being on camera, hosting events; I was constantly burnt out. But the gurus were saying that this is the way business is done, so I kept pushing through even though it felt like holding a beach ball underwater. I thought that if I wanted to be successful, I needed to change. Well, I didn't. If I had wanted to, I would have done it already, after any one of those corporate reviews that insisted that there is no way for someone quiet to get ahead.

While I was writing this book, I interviewed a few introverts – real people, like you and me. When I asked them to complete the sentence 'I'm an introvert so…', everyone started listing the problems that being an introvert created in their lives. Hey, I'm guilty of that too. By default, we think about everything we cannot do by identifying with this personality type.

I'm an introvert so...

... I can't socialise with a group of people.

... I can't walk across the room and introduce myself to a stranger.

... I can't lead a team.

... I can't have a business.

... I can't sell.

And once you tell yourself that you cannot do something, you don't do it. By default, we make it a problem and create fear and anxiety whenever we have to take an action off the 'can't do' list. No one I talked to mentioned the positives until I specifically asked them to. And even then, some of my 'research subjects' went back to talking about the struggles after coming up with one single advantage.

My first breakthrough was deciding to stop making my personality type a problem. I chose to nurture the positive parts of this identity (and there are plenty) and work on the others. I found ways to be successful that are aligned with who I am, and tricks to make the difficult interactions easier. Because as it turns out, you can't ignore people forever. Once I decided to honour who I am, I completely rewrote the story. I stopped telling myself that I'm awkward when I meet someone new, I started practising some of the unavoidable but uncomfortable interactions (like saying no) but I also accepted that some things will never change. I'm sorry, but if something can be said through a text or email, I will never call.

There will always be activities where just the thought of them may make your stomach turn: making phone calls, asking for favours, saying no to those asking something of you, selling, chit-chatting, spending too much time away from home, parties or networking events (especially if they're past your bedtime), being a beginner and going somewhere for the first time, public speaking and probably lots more. However, you must know that there is nothing fundamentally wrong with you. At the same time, you can choose which parts of your identity serve you and you want to keep, and which you would like to upgrade. You wouldn't change because they're wrong, but because you simply want to.

Maybe you want to someday present a TED talk; that means you'll have to work on improving your public speaking skill and that can only happen by practising public speaking. Maybe you really, really want to become a great salesperson; that can only happen if you practise selling. If you want to start a company and be a leader, there is nothing stopping you except for making being an introvert a problem.

You are not broken. Being an introvert is a gift, but society has made us believe that only extroverts have a place in the world. Introverts make amazing leaders. We listen and think things through. We make plans better crafted than anyone else, and because we analyse the world around us quietly, we understand people. We can spot and hire talent and create high-performing teams.

Introverts are highly intelligent. Away from the eyes of the world, we withdraw and study, and invest time in our personal development. Some of the greatest achievements in history were produced by introverts. Albert Einstein, Bill Gates, Steven Spielberg, Sir Isaac Newton, Eleanor Roosevelt, Mark Zuckerberg, Larry Page, J.K. Rowling, Warren Buffett, Mahatma Gandhi, Hillary Clinton, Michael Jordan, Charles Darwin, Meryl Streep, Elon Musk, Dr Seuss, Frederic Chopin, Steve Wozniak, Barack Obama, Emma Watson, Audrey Hepburn... They are only a few of the great people who changed how the world works who have identified as introverts or could be described as such.

Introverts are often kind: we listen, we care and make the world a better place. Introverts are often creative: we love spending time on our own to connect with that creative inner self that needs nurturing, and which, in turn, will produce some of the best art in the world.

For all these reasons, you *can* because you're an introvert. And I already believe that you've got some great achievements under your belt. But yes, I know: there are still some aspects of your personality that will hold you back. The good news is that they are solvable, with a drop of discomfort, a lot of intention and a good goal to aim for.

There are three things that you need to achieve anything: mental energy, physical energy and time. But as introverts, we drain both energy and time by saying yes to everyone else for no other reason than the difficulty of saying no, by spending too much time in the company of others, overthinking and by having a really hard time asking for help.

'But this is who I am; this is who I have been all of my life.' I hear you. I spent my first 30 years saying yes to everyone simply because I felt bad doing otherwise. That only left me with a full to-do list with my own needs at the bottom, a lot of resentment and avoiding social interactions, again to avoid the possibility of someone asking something of me. But I promise you that by the end of this book, you will have changed the story. Because it's all a story in your mind, my friend. We all live a distorted version of reality that we create with our thoughts. Nothing is real unless you believe it is. Let's change the story – it's only a decision.

Let's turn 'I can't because I'm an introvert' into 'I'm the introvert who could'.

PART 1
BOUNDARIES

I promised you from the start that I won't ask you to change, and I will keep my promise. You will improve your people skills if that's your choice, and I have plenty of tips as we progress through the chapters. But my main intention is to help you create the headspace, the time and the energy to do anything you need to do to be successful. As clichéd as it may sound, I want you to be happy.

The next few pages will offer an opportunity for you to design your human interactions – how much, when and with whom – and create boundaries so you can meet your own needs. Maybe you've done this before, but you were unable to enforce those boundaries – you felt guilty, afraid to upset people, and couldn't say no. Don't worry, I've got you. You'll learn how humans think and feel so you can make the best decisions for you no matter what others believe. You'll also learn to say no, which is one of the most difficult habits to learn for any of us.

This will be life changing before you even get to the next parts of the book. You cannot control how others think or behave; you may not even want to change anything about yourself. But what you can do is design an environment and a belief system that are right for you and the life you want to create. No matter what you've been told before, you're not required to play by anyone else's rules. You get to make your own.

The deep-level work you'll do in this part of the book is important. It's magic, even. It will make some problems vanish effortlessly. Instead of trying to fix the surface effects through willpower and force, as you probably did before, you'll solve the root cause. The self-love, self-appreciation and self-esteem that will surface will have you catch yourself thinking 'Wow, who is this person?' while you're confidently delivering a presentation or introducing yourself to someone new without any extra practice of these skills.

Chapter 1
The universal need of all introverts: alone time

The brain gets what the heart wants.

No matter how much other people promote 'getting outside of your comfort zone', for us introverts the comfort zone is where we feel safe, we recover, create and open up. Force an introvert to do things any other way than their way and you won't hear from them ever again. We've been 'ghosting' people before this was even a thing.

One of the most common ways to find comfort is being alone, immersed in activities that might be considered boring by others: reading, doing puzzles, petting the cat or anything else that allows us to hide in the introvert cave. The introvert cave is the ultimate comfort. I call this 'in-between time'. It's when we get to recharge and get ready for another round of 'people time'.

You might often give up (or should I say you're robbed of) that self-connection by your own inability to say no, your friends' pressure to be social a lot more often than you're willing to be, young children that need a lot of attention or work environments that strongly encourage chit-chatting and team-building activities outside of office hours that you feel required to attend. If you ever got to a point where you felt like bursting into tears and desperately wanted to scream 'Leave me alone!', possibly multiple times during the same day, it means you have ignored your needs for too long.

This may be common, but just because it's common doesn't mean it's good for you. You shouldn't reach emotional burnout on a regular basis. You shouldn't be required to function according to someone else's agenda. Your personality type is a trait like any other and it comes with some twists. It's like having freckles. I can bet you've never bullied someone with freckles to stay out in the sun when it might be dangerous only because other people, or even most people, do it. We understand their needs.

When you don't have in-between time

The need to rest, be alone and reconnect with oneself is universal; introverts and extroverts alike feel it, though we value it more. When you have a need that you're unable to meet, your brain will do whatever it can to still get it for you. If you have ever had days of sadness or even depression that forced you to be away from your family for even a few hours and you had no explanation for it, now you do. When you need it, you'll get it no matter what.

I didn't understand this concept until I saw a similar pattern in romantic relationships, where couples who communicate, get along and put a lot of effort into the relationship still fight about seemingly unimportant issues. When one or both partners are busier than usual at work or immersed in a project that requires a lot of their attention, the relationship will lack connection. However, the brain wants what the brain wants (or in this case, the heart). Picking fights will eventually lead to making up, creating connection during a time when it's missing.

Once I became aware of this, I noticed what happened to me when I couldn't get in-between time for self-connection, since for us introverts the most important relationship is with ourselves. Especially since I became a mum, being on my own was a lot more difficult and my brain was always looking for opportunities – good or bad. This went beyond being the first one to volunteer to go to the supermarket. I would pick fights with my husband or even emotionally reject the baby so I would have a good reason to go to my room and be upset for a while. Upset, but alone.

As this was happening, I could see myself changing state and I couldn't stop it. Or I didn't want to. I knew I wouldn't behave as my best self, but at the same time, I craved it so much. There was need, guilt and compassion, all in one single body, and it was exhausting. I came out of it on the other side refreshed but having to make amends. I felt embarrassed and satisfied at the same time. All these contradictory feelings have made me plan downtime a lot more intentionally. I know the consequences if I don't, and I'm not willing to let it get that far.

Creating in-between time

After I left my job in tech, I never missed going to work in an office, but I found myself sometimes missing the commute, even though that was one of the worst parts. Getting off the train in central London was hell on Earth for anyone with anxiety. A sea of overwhelmed people all walking in the same direction continuously between 8 am and 9 am. In the unfortunate event that you needed to go the other way... well, bad luck.

I love not commuting anymore, but I crave it at the same time. That was time to put headphones on and listen to music or read a good book. It was the separation between me and people, whether they were at home, in the office or in the yoga studio. I walked as much of it as I could, and occasionally ran a few miles too.

More and more people are working from home and that might be the case for you too. That's good news: it means you have an extra hour that you can spend on your own. I occasionally go out and work from a coffee shop, or at least take walking breaks, which give me enough energy to go back home and deal with the humans, especially the toddling one.

I understand that if you live with other people, work long hours or have young children, it can feel like there is no in-between. There's only one big chunk of people-time that never breaks. I feel for those mums who can't even be alone in the bathroom. It takes creativity, communication with your partner and letting go of impossible expectations, but it can be done.

I'm lucky I'm married to an introvert who gets me, and we both benefit from asking each other for what we need. Being an introverted mum or dad is difficult, but when both parents feel the need to be alone, the arrangements are easily done. I get Saturday afternoon, he gets Sunday afternoon. I get time to work in the morning, he gets the rest of the day. This schedule didn't happen by accident though. We tried, failed, tried again, found a nanny, readjusted, got the baby into nursery two days a week, then readjusted again, and so on.

I mention these simple ways to be on your own because with the rise of the self-care movement (which I support one hundred per cent), we received the idea that it has to be fancy, expensive or special in some way. That's called an impossible rule, my friend, because you might expect to create a version of it that can never happen due to your circumstances.

There was a season of my life when that aspirational version of self-care was possible. Spa days, club memberships with access to sauna and steam rooms and quick drives to the coast for beach walks were a regular occurrence. Then, once I started working part time, I got every other Friday off work and took my dogs on long walks along the river, followed by a trip to the dog supermarket for them to pick up a new toy. Our doggie version of a girls' day out then ended with a drink at a pet-friendly café and a relaxing walk home. It used to give me a few hours to not-think, get the creative juices flowing again and recharge. And of course, living on a canal boat for two years gave me a lot of solitude time too. That was introvert heaven! I could move on when I didn't like the neighbours, I could pick spots on the river with no other boats and there were big chunks of time when no one walked by.

However, once the baby was born and we moved into a house, I had to let go of the romantic, luxury ideal of the in-between time.

In the current season of my life, reading a book on my own, walking to the coffee shop, those three hours on Saturday afternoon and long walks with the dogs are good enough. Maybe I'll go back to the spa days once the little one goes to school. Or maybe I'll find something even better. But right now, this is good enough.

'But I'm with people *all the time*,' you might say. I bet you're not. You probably have a few minutes every now and then, but the question is... what do you do with them? Run to your phone to open social media? Chat with a friend? Or do you protect those minutes like they're sacred? When they happen, you have control over them, and I challenge you to not give it away. I also challenge you to pay attention to your actions in the next few days and notice what your opportunities for more solitude are.

A few practical tips to make sure you get time to recharge:

→ Brainstorm simple ways to recharge every day, every week and every month. For example, your daily activity might be a meditation or a run; the weekly activity might be going for a walk on a weekend morning or a midweek evening spent reading; the monthly activity can be a whole day off spent doing things you love.

→ If you're constantly skipping your planned in-between time, schedule it in your calendar. As I'm writing this, my favourite weekly way to relax and be on my own is painting. To make sure it happens, I blocked my calendar every Thursday evening from 6 to 8 and I always feel compelled to attend the meeting – it's like a date with myself.

→ Free up more time for yourself by hiring people to offload some house chores. Even having a cleaner for only two hours per week can give you an opportunity for some in-between time, for a very small cost.

→ If you have children, talk to your partner and make arrangements that will benefit both of you; you both deserve some time away from the chaos of a full house. Ask for help from family or friends if needed.

➔ If you ever feel guilty for prioritising yourself, remember that no one benefits from you being unhappy. When you don't take time to recharge, you don't give everything you could be giving, neither at work nor at home. Your brain will still make you take time off, and it's better if you're in control of how that happens.

TAKE ACTION

How can you get some more in-between time? That means intentional, fulfilling and regular time to recharge. How much do you think you need? What are some ways to achieve it in the current season of your life?

THOUGHTS TO PRACTISE

➔ I have the right to take time to recharge.
➔ If I'm better, everyone will benefit from it.

Chapter 2
A quota of interaction

If going through one week is difficult,
you probably can't repeat it forever.
Don't make life impossible.

The truth is, I love being at home. I could spend years without seeing my family (it has happened a few times) or contacting friends. There is however a fine line where, if I cross it, I get too deep into solitude and dip my toes into social anxiety. Once you spend six months without meeting a friend, it becomes really easy to keep going. And once 18 months have passed, it's difficult to push yourself to set up any kind of meet-up. Though I use friends as an example, you can apply this to any type of interaction that you find difficult.

I have to remind myself that I don't want to live alone on a remote island. I couldn't. The world doesn't work like that. There is no way to live a good life without involving anyone else. There's no job that you can do on your own. There's no way to make an impact without collaborating with others. I've met 'loners' and none of them were truly happy, at least not by my definition of happiness. There is no way around this, and both you and I know it; we have to be somewhat social. But there is such a thing as 'too much' and what that is has to be for each one of us to find out because we all have a perfect quota.

If you've been saying to yourself 'I'm an introvert, so I can't be with other people', let's reframe that to 'I'm an introvert AND I can be with other people, in a way that works for me'.

Finding your quota

I don't know about you, but whenever I start something new, I get very excited and occasionally let my emotions interfere with my planning. But feeling full of energy in that moment doesn't mean you'll feel the same when the time comes to do the activity you committed to. It's a lesson you learn the hard way, and I kept learning mine over and over again.

One of those occasions was becoming a full-time coach. It was day one, and I was ready to change the world. With a lot of energy and desire to impact as many people as I could, I knew I had to meet as many people as I could. In that first week, I went to two online networking events, connected with 20 new people and scheduled 12 one-to-one coffee chats. In hindsight... what was I thinking?! While it was a great opportunity to take a leap into my new career, it gave me an insight into how much I can handle before reaching exhaustion.

I should have known this. I had learned it before. Back when I was teaching yoga, by experimenting for a few months I had created a schedule for myself that worked. No matter how tempting it was and how much financial sense it made, I had to respect the boundaries I decided were good for me and say no to adding more regular classes or even covering for other teachers more than a couple of hours per week. If you're too tired to perform, it's best not to do it at all.

To honour your needs and allow plenty of white space to recharge, design your ideal week and, step by step, start to bring it into reality. I know I need days with no human interaction, days without client calls, days without social media and, ideally, days when I can keep my pyjamas on until I go back to bed. As much as possible, I will batch 'front stage' activities because, I have to admit, wearing make-up, dressing up and taking pictures and videos are not on the list of my favourite things.

Finding this balance and the right days for each activity has taken some time to discover. Trial and error. Or should I say: trial, error, tweak and try again. Exceptions will still happen, and some weeks will be complete chaos. Get some rest, reset and then go back to the routine. If going through one week is difficult, you probably can't repeat it forever. Don't make life impossible.

You'd think that having a 9 to 5 job would give you a lot less space to create a comfortable quota, but not anymore. If you have a leading role, you can decide your meetings schedule. If you're an employee or a contractor, you could look at part-time jobs or working from home. The world is going through a transition right now, and flexibility will become increasingly available. In a corporate environment, your relationship with your manager and your team is one aspect you can work on to find more comfort during work hours. Teams are and always will be diverse, and every one of us should be encouraged to continuously improve without changing who we are. Your qualities should be celebrated and used to their fullest potential, but somehow, I've always been on the other end of this situation. I was expected to be loud and social and answer questions without taking some alone time to think.

I want you to consider this: if your manager doesn't understand your needs, it doesn't mean anything about you, but it means everything about their inadequate leadership skills. They didn't take the time to get to know you and don't know yet how you work best. Take ownership of this situation and have a conversation with them. Speaking your mind for a few minutes will be a lot less unpleasant than being outside of your comfort zone for months or even years. Next time when you have an opportunity in your one-to-one meeting, bring up a recent occasion when you weren't comfortable or didn't work optimally, and open up the discussion about your personality. You don't have to label yourself as an introvert; you could just list the implications instead. For example, you might need more than a couple of days to prepare a presentation so you can process your ideas better, or you might not give the best answers when put on the spot. This is great information for your manager to have because if you do your best work, everyone benefits from it. Also, these might not be skills you can work on, but how your brain works.

For those roles with no room for change, prioritising your in-between time is crucial. You might not be able to change your work circum-stances, but know that you can at least decide how much you want to spend with your friends, with non-immediate family, on networking events or on hobbies. I know – some friends will insist on meeting more often. (Don't they know you at all?!) In this case, it's up to you to set some boundaries and enforce them. You might also need to have a conversation with your partner, especially if they're an extrovert; how much you go out, visit families or have family members visit you must be discussed as a team.

You don't 'have to'

There's one more thing though: do you know you don't *have* to meet anyone you don't want to meet? If you've lived a life of 'shoulds' until now, I want to give you permission to drop all of them. Are you doing anything because 'this is how it should be', 'this is how other people do it', 'this is how I grew up', 'this is what adults do', and other assumed obligations? This is a great opportunity to start questioning the reason why you spend time on each one of your relationships. Putting up boundaries is less about the other person and more about how you want to treat yourself. It's less about what the other person will think, and more about designing your life as you desire. If there were no regrets and no one got hurt, who would you stop spending time with?

When I was a teenager, my mum used to drag me along with her to visit family when all I really wanted was to stay at home. Sometimes I wanted to read or do homework, and she still forced me to go 'because they're family and you have to be there'. I never understood why 'I have to'. Once we got there, of course, I wanted to rest in a corner and silently watch TV. 'Come on, come talk to us, don't be so shy!' was among the first things I heard after our arrival, followed by an eye roll and a comment towards Mum about how I'll never be successful if I don't get more confident and vocal. But you know what I'm going to say: it had nothing to do with confidence. I was happy in my quietness. It wasn't shyness; it was a desire for recharging. I wanted to not be there, or at least be left alone with my own thoughts for a while. Just as it still is now, my mind was my happy place. You're not a teenager anymore; you can choose to say no to an invitation, and no one will drag you along against your will.

Your ideal friend avatar

Just like calories, not all people have been created equal. Some are nurturing and some are energy draining. No quota will make up for the fact that you don't enjoy someone's company. You need people and people skills, but it's not your responsibility to accept all people, no matter what. When I had a friend who I genuinely loved and wanted to spend time with, I was comfortable being with them all the time. While this was harder to achieve as I got older, I still believe that I can be both an introvert and have people in my life I want to spend a lot of time with. The quality of those people matters though. And maybe you cannot change your family, but you can absolutely change your friends.

Whenever I'm in environments with people who share my hobbies, values or interests, meeting them becomes easy. I want to be there. I want to chat with them. Yes, I need a small push to follow through with my plan and get to the event/location/online meeting room, but once I give myself a quick pep talk and go for it, I never regret it. (Side note: if, hours ahead of the event, you dread the interaction even if you were very excited about it when you planned it, you're not alone. I do this all the time. And it's really good to know this about yourself. When the moment comes, you'll know it's normal. You do it all the time. And you also know you'll feel great afterwards.)

Find your people and being with them will feel easy. Love books? Join a book club. Have a business? Join a mastermind group for entrepreneurs or go to meet-ups. Like writing? Join a writing community. The first interaction will still feel uncomfortable, but you know right from the start that you have a lot in common.

In business, there's something called the ideal client avatar. It's a detailed description of the person who would benefit from your services *and* would be a pleasure to work with. You think about their traits, thoughts, problems, etc. I recommend doing the same with friends. Design your ideal friend avatar – what hobbies do they have? Where do they hang out? What kind of qualities do they have?

You're not required to like everyone, and you're allowed to invest more time in those relationships that feed your soul and drop the ones that drain your emotional and mental energy. That friend who keeps complaining. The co-worker that gossips. The negative Twitter account. Buh-bye!

You might not be able to design and pick your family, but you can design and pick your friends. Decide you no longer need to apologise for wanting quality people in your life, needing time alone or doing things your way.

TAKE ACTION

→ What would a first draft of your ideal week look like? How would you organise your days in a way that gives you enough time when you're not required to be visible?

→ Define your ideal friend avatar.

→ Declutter your online social environment. Leave groups you've outgrown, unfollow people that don't make you feel good about yourself or don't add value to your life, and unsubscribe from emails you're not interested in reading anymore.

→ Think about the boundaries you'd like to set with friends or family. How much is too much? The next few chapters will help you not only feel better about boundaries, but also to set and enforce them.

THOUGHTS TO PRACTISE

→ I get to choose who I spend time with, and how much.

→ I'm an introvert *and* I can be with other people, in a way that works for me.

→ I no longer apologise for wanting quality people in my life.

Chapter 3
How humans think, feel and experience life

Every one of us lives in our own version of reality. A distorted version. At times, it doesn't even matter what the facts are – what matters is how you decide to see them.

On many occasions, your difficulty in getting the words out in a social setting, approaching someone or with enforcing your boundaries (saying no) is partly because you don't want to cause a negative reaction. You want them to like you (#peoplepleasing); you don't want to hurt someone's feelings or, even worse, have them think you're stupid. But how every human reacts depends only on their own identity. It depends on what their values are, their belief system, thoughts, energy and experiences. No matter what you do or what you say, how they choose to respond is entirely up to them.

Although you can purposefully and skilfully influence other people's actions (as you'll see in future chapters), it's not something that we employ in our day-to-day lives with family, friends and even co-workers. This is a truth that you have to live with: you can't change someone's identity, hence you cannot change how they think or feel about you or what you do. How they react is their decision and it frees you from the need to control. Whether they like what you say or not – it's their business. Whether they like you or not – their business. How someone responds to something you say, or to you saying nothing at all – their business. You get to be, do and say everything you want, and they will respond based on who they are, their own experiences and the lens they see life through.

A few years ago, I went back home to visit my mum and took her out for lunch to an Italian restaurant. I glanced over at the waitress and thought to myself, 'Oops, she doesn't look happy'. The menu was huge, so Mum took a while to decide what she was going to have. Plus, we hadn't seen each other in more than a year so we had a lot to catch up on. It took a while. The waitress came to take our order after only a couple of minutes, and we asked for more time. The next time she came by to check if we were ready she was in a much more negative state than before. We asked for a couple more minutes and she almost snapped, saying nothing but gesturing something to let us know that she'd had enough of us annoying, time-wasting customers.

I thought nothing of it. I knew right from the beginning that this wasn't about us. She was either upset about something that had happened to her that day or that's who she simply was. Mum felt rushed to make a decision: 'Let me just pick something; it looks like I've upset her.' But that wasn't true. For all I knew, we could have been the perfect customers and the waitress would still have been upset. Even if we had made a decision in the first couple of minutes, maybe she would still have snapped. More people came to the restaurant; she behaved the same with all of them and, statistically, at least some of them knew what they wanted to eat more quickly than we did.

The time came to leave the table, and a tip, and I found myself overthinking. What if I leave a big tip and she thinks she did a great job, even if she didn't? But what if I don't leave a big tip and she thinks 'Of course they didn't – I knew it' or 'That's why I hate this job', and this perpetuates her behaviour? But just as I had no idea what thoughts she had during the whole interaction with us, I couldn't make any assumptions now either. I cannot read other people's minds, so all I can do is watch my own thoughts and make my own decisions based on what I know. I went for the standard tip I always leave. It wasn't my job to make her day worse, or better. I couldn't, because that's her responsibility. The only thing I could do was not respond to her negativity with even more hate, not be a jerk and pay for her service as I thought best.

Knowing that her feelings were in no way created by anything that I'd said or done, I went on with my day thinking nothing of it anymore. But what did create her feelings? The restaurant, the job, a previous customer, something that happened to her on her way to work? Just as I didn't cause her anger, neither did all these different situations. Her feelings were caused by her interpretation of the situation, her belief system and her own energy. If she was thinking 'I hate my job', then us asking for more time to decide was only confirming what she already believed. If she was focusing on her unhappy energy, she was constantly scanning the environment for more proof that life indeed sucks, and we gave her a little. Who knows what atrocious requests other tables had? A slice of lemon for the sparkling water or, even worse, an extra set of cutlery because the toddler at table 6 didn't listen and dropped his fork on the floor, even though his mum told him repeatedly to stop playing with it?

You can't make anyone feel anything. If that wasn't true, the world would be chaos; there would be no free will. Knowing this brings with it a lot of freedom. If your people-pleasing comes from a desire to make the other person feel good, there's one less responsibility on you. And if it's coming from your desire to feel good, you can now understand that you can make that happen without involving anyone else.

Same event, different interpretations

Each human lives in their own bubble of beliefs and energy. The world outside your bubble keeps going and going, but has no effect on you unless you pay attention to it and make your own interpretation. Your experience still happens on the inside; however, the actions you take can produce an effect in the outside environment. The changes in the world can then be interpreted by another bubble, but the two of you are still 100 per cent independent. Also, the two of you can look at one single aspect of the world outside and have different interpretations based on your different inner worlds.

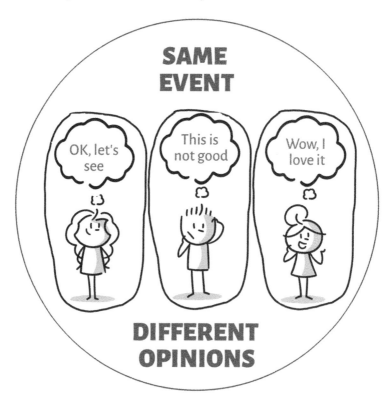

This became obvious to a lot more people when the Covid-19 pandemic started in early 2020. Life was mostly the same for everyone. Though the details varied from country to country, all of us experienced lockdowns and changes in routine, environment, income. How each individual reacted was different, and some managed to get through it a lot better than others.

There were those who saw an opportunity to rest more, start a business, invest in the stock market, have sex every day on company time, read more, learn about their children's education, learn to cook, play an instrument or enjoy not having to commute. There were those who felt that their freedom was taken away, organised online happy hours to drink gin at two in the afternoon, wished that every day went by faster, spent hours watching the news to feed their anxiety and whose minds were constantly fogged by thoughts such as 'it's unfair', 'this is a disaster', 'I can't do this any longer'. And of course there were those who unfortunately couldn't cope. Along with the deaths from the virus, we saw a rise in deaths caused by physical abuse, suicide and drugs. The world outside our bubbles was similar, but we all felt differently.

'It's so stressful,' someone said to me.

'What is?' I asked.

'This whole situation.'

I wasn't stressed, which meant her statement couldn't have been true. If it wasn't stressful for everyone, it means it can't be stressful by default. It also means that something can't be fundamentally one way or another. It just is. And then you make up your own mind about how you want to see it.

I'd be lying if I told you I didn't have any moments of anxiety or any other emotional pain. I felt sad that I was 20 weeks pregnant and realised I wasn't going to go to any classes, to meet other mums-to-be or even see my own mum for the entirety of this phase of life. I felt sad that I had to say goodbye to my boat way before we had planned to, after it being our home for almost two years. I occasionally felt frustrated that everything was more complicated than it used to be. Every time that happened, I watched my thoughts and allowed myself to feel how I felt for a little while, knowing that it would pass if I let it be.

But most of the time, I focused on the positives and grabbed each opportunity that came my way. Lockdown… was fun. I lived by the sea, had a lot of time with my husband and dogs ahead of the baby being born, grew a business, ate loads of tasty foods, started a few self-care habits, and all in all, life was good. That was my bubble, and it seemed like everyone was very protective of their own.

But who's right?

As a rule I created for myself, I never comment on social media posts about controversial topics, the pandemic being one, but I like to scan through other people's comments to understand different points of view (and let's be honest, to entertain myself). There were mostly two different camps and each of them supported their own views and fought against the other. Never, ever, have I seen someone switching camps, no matter how compelling the arguments or how nicely they were presented. For each of them, the truth was their own, and nothing else mattered. The comments confirming their truth were reacted to with hearts and hugs, and all the others were bombarded with the anger and tears emojis.

So who's right? No one, and everyone. Each opinion feels like the truth for the human expressing it. With the information they have in the moment, their life experiences and beliefs, that's what feels like the most logical conclusion. Each one of us lives in our own version of reality. A distorted version even. At times, it doesn't even matter what the facts are – what matters is how you decide to see them.

Just as you can't convince a stranger on the internet to change their mind about lockdowns or vaccines, you can't control someone's reaction to what you say or do. All you can do is choose the best for yourself, while being as nice as possible, and give them a chance to respond based on the state of their own bubble. It would be a waste of time and energy to go through all the possible scenarios in your mind, overprepare or even make a commitment against your will, only to get a less than ideal reaction. You can't upset or disappoint anyone; those are feelings that belong to them and over which you have no control. And if they experience disappointment, that doesn't make you a bad person because they choose to feel disappointment. Yes, it's a choice. How you feel and react in the moment is due to what you're thinking, the story you're creating in your mind about the situation. And that, if you're aware of it, can be changed.

Even if you disappoint someone, you're not a bad person. You're just a person who said or didn't say words, or took or didn't take an action, that someone else made an interpretation of. And if that someone likes you or not, there's nothing you can do to guarantee they will change their mind. And you're still neither good nor bad. You just are.

I love puppies, and if you're in the same camp as me, it will come as a big surprise that not everyone does. I see children on the street running away when I walk my dogs. Someone almost had a panic attack on a train because I sat next to them with my beagles. But there are also plenty that come to pet them and happily watch them perform tricks in exchange for some chicken breast. (Two dogs spinning or rolling at the same time is adorable!) With so many people that like them and so many that don't, how do you decide if they're good or bad? You don't. They're not good or bad; they just are. Nothing is fundamentally good or bad; it just is. And so are you. Thankfully, puppies don't make any interaction mean anything about them. They move on with their day and on to the next bush that needs to be sniffed. Not having a human brain serves them well in many situations.

In any interaction with another human, there are three versions of the story: theirs, yours and the facts. You now know that it's very unlikely you can influence the other person's version. Plus it gives you extra responsibility, and haven't you had enough of that already? Don't you want to let everyone be who they are so you can be who you are too? And that leaves you with your own story, which you are the writer of, and so you can change it as you please.

While still being as considerate and polite as you can, say what you want to say and be quiet when that's what you want. Be who you want to be. And let the rest of the world do the same.

THOUGHTS TO PRACTISE

➔ I can't change how people react to what I say or do; I might as well do what's best for me.

➔ I'm not a bad person if I choose to do what's best for me.

➔ If someone doesn't like me, it has nothing to do with me.

➔ My feelings are always my responsibility.

➔ I'm not responsible for someone else's feelings – they are.

Chapter 4
Saying no without guilt

When you live believing that you're not good enough, everything you do is a desperate act to become so. Every yes is an opportunity to prove yourself to others, and yourself.

My first confident 'No' was by no means a life-changing decision. Though my personal development journey helped me to eventually be protective of my schedule or ask for what I want in a business negotiation, my breakthrough happened when I bravely yet politely declined a keychain.

My husband and I were having lunch at Planet Hollywood in Disneyland Paris and while we were waiting for food, one of the waiters, momentarily turned photographer, asked if we wanted a picture. I said yes to the picture, genuinely interested in getting a print because we rarely get quality pictures as a couple. I should mention, though, that we had just run a half marathon a few hours beforehand, so we were tired and hungry.

The prints came 15 minutes later – an A5 image, plus a keychain and a magnet. What a disappointment. We looked exactly how we felt after our run through the magical kingdom, and that was not an image I wanted to be displayed in my living room, let alone on my fridge (I see that very often). 'Wow, this is it. This is the moment,' I thought. I felt a rush of adrenaline and all the emotions at once: anxiety, excitement and pride. My brain started playing the default soundtrack:

'What if they get upset?'

'I'm not brave enough.'

'But it's rude, it's a waste, the work is already done!'

And then, in an instant, like stopping a broken record with that squeaky, shuffle sound, I replaced the voice in my head with: 'I can do this. I'm going to say no.'

Without an ounce of guilt, I refused the prints, having been told in the beginning that it was an option. We weren't expected to buy them if we didn't love them, and we didn't love them. There was more to celebrate during that meal than our completed run, as I was now the proud owner of another (imaginary) medal: Introvert of the Year, only awarded to those capable of refusing merchandise sold via questionable, pressuring and guilt-inducing techniques. In that moment, Disneyland was indeed the happiest place on Earth.

Though the keychain might not have been a big deal, it's a great reminder that not being comfortable saying no extends to more than just tasks and meetings that overcrowd your schedule and suck your energy. You'll see it in your bank account, draining your hard-earned cash, through direct debits to charities that maybe you're not that supportive of, and courses, programs or products that were sold through a direct pitch you couldn't avoid. Well, you might be so busy you have no personal time to spend the money on something better anyway, but it's still nice to have it.

And let's not forget about the useless objects cluttering the house because you couldn't refuse gifts, and all the extra food that was eaten throughout the years because it's rude to say no. I know it's easy to say yes. It's nice to be liked. You wouldn't want to upset anyone, be in a confrontation or have them think you don't care. Plus, sometimes you don't even have a good reason to say no, and you just want to get those people off your back. Sometimes, you're not even given the chance to say yes or no.

But enough is enough. Let's do something about it. Because here's what saying yes does to your schedule and energy.

The effects of saying yes

Do a simple exercise with me. You'll need your to-do list and a calendar, ideally with a weekly spread.

Add on the list everything you need to get done next week and estimate how long it will take you. Add everything from commute time, shopping trips, coffee with your best friend to work-related projects. Before even adding them to your calendar, analyse your list and answer this question for each of the items: who is this for? Will the outcome be beneficial for me or for someone else?

Do I really want to do this or did I commit to it out of guilt or people-pleasing?

Circle those that are for you in green and the rest in red. Add them to your calendar, and if possible, keep the colours – green for you, red for others. What's the predominant colour on your calendar? Who's taking up the most space? And after everything has been laid out in a physical space, how much is it still left? Is there any other slot that you can take with a green task? Do you still have enough space in your life for your own goals?

When you're saying yes to something you don't want to do, it's not only the activity itself that will drain your energy but also the overthinking about it that happens days in advance. Plus, you probably didn't calendar the in-between time you'll need to recover afterwards. Even trying to get out of something you said yes to but later changed your mind about can mentally exhaust you. A phone call can turn into hours of rehearsal, then procrastination, then finally picking up the phone and letting it ring twice, expecting the other end to answer quickly but hanging up when they don't, pacing around, calling again, having the two-minute conversation and then having to take a walk around to calm down the buzzing sensation going around in your body.

What I want you to see is that commitments come with conse-quences and there's more to a coffee chat with a friend than the hour spent in their company. You learn to respect your time a lot more when you realise that if you keep offering it to others, there isn't enough left for you. That's when you at least start to desire to say no more, even though it still feels like something impossibly hard to do. That desire will continue to grow as you set a goal that you need time and energy for, and you see that each yes to someone else is a no to yourself.

Rude or empowering?

I grew up in a culture where saying no was not well received by parents or teachers. It was considered rude, defiant even. I remember it being one of my favourite words growing up, or at least this was one of my father's most common complaints. But telling a child that refusing is equal to misbehaving, and misbehaving is equal to punishment, will eventually convince them to stop.

Saying yes was a part of growing up, and the more obedient, the better. It makes sense why our parents wanted us to always agree with all their requests. The less independent we were, the more control they had. And since adults believe they know best, control meant we would be good students, go to college, get a job, get married to a good partner and have well-behaved children of our own.

For the most part, it worked. Many of us lived the safe life that was designed by our parents. But was it a happy one? For some, yes. But for others, the spell wears off when they realise they don't even know how they got to where they are. They feel like a puppet that suddenly gets a heart and a brain and decides to break free, to spend the rest of their days in a more fulfilling way.

Undoing decades of docility takes time and awareness. It requires you to look deep within and decide which story you want to believe.

That saying no is rude? Or that it's empowering? Don't worry, you won't have to go to therapy with your parents, or even confront them. You won't need to go through any rituals of forgiveness in which you burn photos or cross spears through dolls' hearts. You won't need to be hypnotised to remember each and every event that you need to heal from. The past is the past and it cannot be changed. Though it's helpful to understand where one of your traits is coming from, there's no need to look back again and again. It's the future that matters.

Already good enough

But there's something more to saying yes – it's another opportunity to prove yourself to other people, and to yourself. When you live believing that you're not good enough, everything you do is a desperate act to become so. This is also a belief that we grow up with, learned from our lovingly ignorant parents and teachers, who thought that setting impossible standards would turn us into ambitious, successful people.

Even if it did, the negative consequences are there too. No matter how much we take on, how much we work, how much we sacrifice, it's never enough.

When I was a child, no matter how much I cleaned my room, it was never clean enough. No matter what I cooked, it wasn't good enough. So what if I got good grades if I wasn't going to win the Math Olympiad (I only came second in my county)? At the end of the day, I was always falling short, and the next day was yet another attempt to get a 'well done', which was really hard to come by.

It was a moving target. I could never stop and enjoy what I had because the next step was already in front of me, waiting to be taken. Yes, it turned me into an achiever, but at the same time, it stopped me from living in the present.

Unfortunately, the present is where you exist, and always looking at the next destination makes it not good enough. It makes *you* not good enough. This never ends, unless you decide to put a stop to it. It's a pleasure to achieve goals and get better and better, but the motivation behind it needs to change. Striving to be better because you're not good enough comes with endless suffering, people-pleasing, sacrifice, and wishing for every day to pass faster so you can get to the next one, work more and get to a future that promises to be better. And it never is.

Once you decide you're a complete and deserving human being already, goals are fun; they are a way towards self-actualisation. That is a different kind of energy, with a different kind of result. You love life and what you do in every moment, while already feeling successful and proud of yourself.

Skills can be developed, fitness can be improved, relationships can get better, if you want them to. As a professional or integral part of a team, you can up your game. But as a human, you are already good enough; learn to make the distinction.

Have your own back

Starting to say no has to be one of the most difficult, yet freeing habits. It means you acknowledge your own desires and trust yourself to make the decisions that are best for you. You're gaining back control over your life and over the consequences of your choices. It's empowering and scary at the same time. When you won't let someone else tell you what to do, you don't have anyone else to blame either. Good or bad, the decision is yours.

One of the consequences you will have to deal with is the other person's reaction, and standing your ground no matter what that is. Ideally, you'll be met by a simple 'OK!'. The worst scenario is them throwing a tantrum and not speaking to you anymore. But of course, in most cases, it will be something in between. What do you want to believe regardless of the reaction? Here are a few helpful thoughts to practise:

- → 'How they feel has nothing to do with me.'
- → 'I made the best decision for myself.'
- → 'It's a pity that I can't help, but now is not the right time.'

→ 'On this particular occasion, I have to choose myself.'

→ 'Being a good friend has nothing to do with how much I do for others.'

→ 'I'm really sorry they're upset; I wish they would be more understanding of my needs.'

In some situations, it's useful to put yourself in the requester's shoes. Do you believe that a good friend is always required to say yes? Would you understand if one of your requests was denied? Do you only appreciate your friends for what they do for you? If that's the case, is that even a friendship? And if it isn't a friendship, why do you care so much?

You don't need a reason to say no

Another common, faulty belief is that you need a reason to say no. For most of my life, I spent unreasonable amounts of time and energy coming up with 'valid' excuses to get out of commitments. Adding guilt about lying on top of the guilt of disappointing others caused even more overthinking. Thankfully, life was kind enough at times to give me the headache I lied about so I could truthfully spend Friday night at home, in pain, but with a clean conscience. It was so exhausting that saying yes felt like the easier way out.

But this is based on the foundational belief that it's wrong to say no. If this was a satisfactory, acceptable response, then you wouldn't need a reason. 'No' is enough, though it won't feel like it for a long time. You'll find yourself either blurting out an excuse, or at least softening the blow by adding 'Sorry' or 'I can't', even though you intellectually understand that you don't need to. It's OK not to try to go straight from 'Unfortunately, I can't attend because my cat is having a birthday party' to 'No' by going through 'I can't tonight, but I'll see you next time', 'Unfortunately I can't attend today, but you guys have fun', or 'My schedule is stretched out so I can't help'.

You need to find a reply that feels true and is helping you act in alignment with your own desires and way of being.

When they don't need you

If you're trying to walk in the shoes of the other person, you'll see that many times what they need is a solution to their problem, but the solution doesn't necessarily have to come from you. When you need your grocery shopping done, you don't care if it shows up to your door through a delivery, you use the click-and-collect service, someone else from the household goes to do the shopping or you do. All you want is the shopping to be done. Similarly, when someone asks something of you, you can interpret 'Can you help me with this?' to mean 'Can you or someone you know help me or redirect me to someone that can?'

You don't hold all the answers of the universe and you're not expected to.

One of my friends, knowing that I'm passionate about health and fitness and at the same time that I'm not a doctor, asked for my opinion regarding a health issue she was experiencing. I wanted to be the best friend possible, and started searching online for the problem. Like an out-of-body experience, I watched myself being desperate to give an answer on the spot, on a topic I knew nothing about, even if at that moment I was engaged in another activity. 'What are you doing?' I asked myself. 'She probably already searched; she's a smart girl.'

I truthfully told her that it's outside my area of expertise, but I know of a doctor that might offer advice related to some of the symptoms she was describing. I gave her the name and the website and asked her to keep me in the loop. A few weeks later, I followed up with her to see how she was feeling because that is my real role as a friend.

Recognise when you are not the best person for the job, and if possible, recommend someone who is. Not only are you staying out of trouble by not giving bad advice or offering a poor service, but you'll really help that person by allowing an expert to get the job done in a way that will serve your friend better.

The golden rule

You're also not the best person for the job when you don't want to do it. If you're not passionate about it, it's not aligned with your goals or your schedule is stretched to the max, the result will not be your best work. If you're saying yes from a desire to not disappoint yourself or others, sometimes that is exactly the result you'll create. It's impossible to create a piece of art when you don't have the focus, the energy or the motivation to do it. And so, acting from fear – 'What if they get upset?', 'I don't want to feel guilty for saying no', 'What if I'm not good enough?' – will usually lead to manifesting that fear into reality. If the result is not your best work, they will be upset, you will feel guilty and it won't be good enough.

This leads me to the golden rule when deciding whether it's a yes or a no: 'No to fear, yes to love.'

The reason behind accepting a task, a day out or doing someone a favour needs to be positive and rooted in abundant energy. Here are a few examples:

Reasons rooted in fear:

- → I need to prove that I'm good enough.
- → I don't want to upset them.
- → What if they stop talking to me if I say no?
- → I'll feel guilty if I don't do it.
- → Who am I to say no?

Reasons rooted in (self-)love:

- → I'll do it because I want to.
- → It's aligned with my goals, so I will happily take it on.
- → I'll go out because I can't wait to see them!
- → This will help me improve the skills I'm working on.
- → I see this having a positive impact on my life.

You could argue that every one of those reasons is positive. Not wanting to be a bad friend, not wanting to disappoint: those sound like something a good person would do. While that is true, those reasons are rooted in fear, which is a negative type of energy.

The impact of saying yes might also be negative: frustration, overworking, burnout. Apply the golden rule and have your own back after making the decision.

The need for significance and connection

While the energy might be negative, the intention behind everything you do is positive. If your mind didn't believe that it was right, you wouldn't do it. For example, when you act out of fear, your brain believes it's protecting you. Even when the result is detrimental, if the action helps you meet a basic need, then it will feel critical for you to take it.

One of those needs is significance. The feeling that you're important, your actions matter and you're in some way special. All humans have this need, and all humans meet it in one way or another, good or bad. Saying yes to every single request that comes your way can be a form of seeking significance, even if you don't consciously recognise it. If they keep coming to you for help, they need you, and it feels good to be needed. The more you help, the more they'll come back and the more they'll need you. And so you end up in a vicious cycle you can't break.

You even complain about it. You say you're frustrated that your schedule is full, or that you're not in the mood to spend another weekend with your friend going through a rough patch. Still, you do it anyway. Because they need you. But remember, they don't always need *you*, they need their problem solved, and there are others that can do it too.

Another need closely related to our topic is connection. We all crave human love and connection, and it's the oldest need of the human race, apart from the basic, physiological ones. It's independent of personality type, as humans cannot survive alone. While the species was still evolving, being in a group kept you safe and was your best chance of getting food, shelter or escape from danger.

Being an introvert doesn't change our desire for deep relationships. We may have fewer than others, but the ones we have, we treasure.

The fear of being alone and unloved is primal; it's part of the default software your brain comes with. We may function differently to others when it comes to interactions, but we still feel the need to have friendships, romantic relationships, talk, and feel supported, loved and understood. But just as with the need for significance, there are two sides of the coin, and this can sometimes come up disguised as people-pleasing.

But now you know what you need to ask yourself: is this rooted in love or in fear? is this something I want or something I feel I have to do? Spending quality time with someone, being supportive, thinking of them, sending them positive thoughts are all good ways to meet your need for connection. Sacrifice is not.

Dependency

I know that most times when you say yes, you genuinely want to help. But what if what's best for the other person at that moment is for you to allow them to problem-solve on their own? When you repeatedly help with an issue, you create dependency; the person becomes unable and possibly unwilling to try to do it themselves. You are, essentially, an enabler.

They become powerless to solve the issue themselves and hand their responsibility for their emotions and actions over to you. Adults should be able to handle disappointment, fear or anger and take ownership of their life. No matter how difficult it might be, the best you can do for someone else at times is to say no. It won't feel good! However, feeling negative emotions doesn't mean the decision is wrong. Many great choices in life will be painful and good for you at the same time.

No is a filtering system

I'm married to a hardcore introvert. Before I met him, I didn't believe there was someone in the world more introverted than myself. Any tiny sign that you might invade his privacy or one single alarm bell about you needing something from him, and he shuts down. It's understandable though. After years of being taken advantage of, you intuitively start to put some boundaries up. My husband got his Introvert of the Year award a few months after my keychain rejection success, after he turned down a network marketing 'opportunity'.

It was a Sunday morning, we had a four-month-old baby and desperately needed rest. With both of us working full time at home raising the little one, the weekends were a breath of fresh air after juggling a complex schedule Monday to Friday. Each one of us had big goals. We knew exactly what we wanted out of life; we were laser focused and working our sleep-deprived asses off.

Someone who we hadn't talked to in a while asked us if we wanted to chat and we happily said yes. For all we knew, we were meeting a friend for a virtual coffee that morning. It all turned into a sales pitch that was unexpected, hence unavoidable, and due to respect for the friend pitching, we both watched it until the end, occasionally planting seeds of refusal. Though my husband concluded the meeting saying he was not interested, another text was needed a week later to confirm his intentions.

It wasn't only a test for the internal work he's been doing, but also another proof of what saying yes can cause: your own priorities and goals go to the bottom of the list, especially when you don't have full clarity on what those are. When you know what you want, you intuitively know what you don't. Your goal becomes the lens through which you filter every opportunity that comes your way. Some will be a hard pass, some will be a 'hell yeah', and some will be somewhere in the middle.

That day when my husband said no to the network marketing business, here's what he told me: 'I had so much clarity about where I want our lives to go that I had no doubt in my mind. I didn't need to think about it. I didn't even want to waste my energy by saying I'll come back with an answer later. I wanted it to end then and there, so I can go back and continue the work I'm meant to do.' When you have certainty, even when you don't yet see the whole path ahead, you can at least decide what the 'hell no's are. On that day, for us, the 'opportunity' was a 'hell no'.

No matter what you do, the world will stay exactly the same. Sales representatives will use the same tried and tested methods to make you buy, charity workers will always try to stop you on the street to ask you to commit to a monthly donation, your mum will always offer more food, and many others will always have requests from you. You cannot stop them. With some, mostly those you know well and interact with often, you can build and train boundaries, but for most of the world, things will always be the same.

The only thing that you can do is change how you think, how you react, what you expect from each interaction, and make the best decision for yourself. Then, you too will earn that magical Introvert of the Year medal, every year, for the rest of your life.

TAKE ACTION

Here's a simple script you can use to say no in a polite but confident way:

1. Start by acknowledging the request: 'I appreciate you thinking of me'; 'Thank you for considering me for this'.
2. Say no: 'I'm unavailable at this time'; 'I'm unable to take this on'; 'I'd rather not'.
3. If you really want to, give a reason, but practise without it too.
4. Offer an alternative or a resource if you have one. 'I know someone that might help you', 'I can recommend a resource', 'I wrote a blog post about it', 'I heard about this topic in...'
5. If it's a friend or a family member and you want to show you care, follow up after a few days or weeks to see how they're getting on.

THOUGHTS TO PRACTISE

→ I'm good enough. I can stop proving myself to others.

→ I can choose to pause and believe that I'm good enough even if I need to rest.

→ I'm good enough even if I make mistakes.

→ I'm good enough even if sometimes life is hard and I can't cope.

→ I'm good enough even if I can't do everything for everybody.

→ I'm good enough even if I don't yet know everything.

→ I'm good enough even if I need to ask for help.

→ I'm good enough and human at the same time. I have my limits and they don't make me any less worthy or complete.

→ I don't need a reason to say no.

→ I don't have all the answers and that's OK.

→ A yes to someone else is a no to myself.

→ Being a good friend has nothing to do with how much I do for others.

Chapter 5
A 'how' that works for you

---

*Your creation can be what everyone
else sees, without ever needing to know
the person behind it.*

I started my first online business by accident. My friends kept asking me questions about my diet and my exercise routine, and I got tired of repeating myself. A blog poorly named 'Penny Plain Fit' started from a desire to share words that I never thought would be read by people other than my closest friends. But as I wrote more, I got better at writing and as I got better at writing, more people noticed. Though I was now technically an influencer, the most visible and intrusive activity was having my picture taken.

I felt at ease writing and minimally interacting with people. The blog life was a great life. But when the time came to grow, I had to promote myself in different ways, or so I believed. Back then, webinars were just becoming very popular and the business mentor whom I was learning from at that moment, who was also curiously an introvert, made a good case for hosting a webinar.

'The discomfort is temporary,' he said.

'If you need to promote yourself you need to get out there,' he said.

'And while you're launching your product, go live on your social media platforms,' he said.

Now when I look back, I realise he wasn't doing that. Ah, the irony.

For the sake of growth and getting myself outside of the dreaded comfort zone that apparently kills dreams, I did it. I started organising webinars because I thought that was the way. It felt horrible. I did it again. It felt horrible again. The anxiety eventually disappeared; he was right in that respect. I got more and more used to being in front of the camera, and doing live videos and presentations. Though I wasn't nervous anymore, it still felt like I didn't belong. At the risk of plaguing the page with overused words, I felt 'out of alignment'. 'If this is what it takes to grow a business,' I thought, 'then maybe business is not for me.'

I had no problem recording a video or a presentation; I love teaching. But I wanted to take my time preparing and recovering afterwards. I preferred Q&As rather than interactive workshops, podcasts versus video, and one-to-one coaching versus groups. However, if I had to choose one thing to do for the rest of my life, it would have been writing. It always felt good, authentic, and it allowed me to serve people without putting make-up on (urgh, exhausting!) or changing out of my comfy clothes.

I chose the path of least resistance and started focusing my promotion on email. I recorded classes, created PDFs and even a course, without ever interacting with anyone. From then on, I developed my email writing and storytelling skills and have made email my main way of communicating with my community. The next step for me was recording a podcast, which also felt very introvert friendly, but required more effort. I had to talk, after all. My lazy ass fell back to writing after 25 episodes.

Now, three years later, I do all of it, but at a frequency that feels good for me and gets me excited instead of exhausted. I do what feels fun and keeps me in the creative comfort zone. When I have the energy to do a live video on social media and I feel the pull to do it, I do it. If weeks pass by without showing up on camera at all, I'm OK with that too. So far, I have managed to keep the balance between respecting my energy and showing my face enough that people will know and trust me.

There will always be some ways to express yourself that work better than others – try to focus on those. It's worth repeating that if you're working a 9 to 5, your manager should spend time getting to understand you and help you shine.

Knowing that there isn't only one right way to achieve your goal, how would you do it in a way that is aligned with who you are? What do you enjoy doing? Can you do more of that and less of those activities that you feel a lot of resistance towards?

Just as it was for me, some of those uncomfortable activities are unavoidable. When that's the case, the story you tell yourself matters. One of my stories used to be 'I'm awkward when I meet someone new'. I repeated that in my mind so many times that not only it was true, but it made me avoid meeting new people. In case you didn't know it yet, this is not good for business.

The first step is to drop the story, or at least recognise it for what it is – sentences you keep repeating in your mind. I decided to stop telling myself I'm awkward and wrote a better, more positive story: I'm a lovely person and people are lucky to know me. Plus, when I know I'm there for someone else's benefit and it's not about me at all, I can switch off my overthinking brain and serve.

The story you've been telling yourself is just that – a story that is reinforcing an action you keep taking (or not taking). But remember, nothing is true or false unless you decide it is. You live in your own altered version of reality, and you can add a plot twist whenever you want to.

Creator vs performer

Even if the first part of this chapter was about being literally visible – showing your face and meeting people – there is one more way for the world to know you, and that's through your work. Your creation can be what everyone else sees, without ever needing to know the person behind it. This can be true for artists (painters, writers, etc.), but you can be the invisible master from behind the scenes in many roles.

I realised this as I was picking up a book from the shelf and told myself: 'I have no idea what the author looks like.' Yes, some books or other masterpieces were created such a long time ago that photographs didn't even exist, so it's impossible to have a clear image of the people who brought them out into the world. But the book I'm referring to was published only five years ago. Even though I read and re-read it, I was never interested in knowing the person behind it. I don't need to.

After I started painting, having already written the book, my husband asked me: 'What's next for you in the area of creativity? Would you like to learn how to sing maybe?' I started laughing at the thought of my voice, which is definitely something to make fun of. But that's not why I said, 'Oh, no, no, no.' When you perform, you are the product; singing would mean that all eyes are on me. It made me look back at my work, my businesses and all my hobbies. I prefer to create, not to perform. It's one of the reasons why I don't teach yoga anymore. It's why writing feels effortless. It's why my first ever business was selling crocheted baby hats. It's why the second one was blogging. It's why I love to plan events but hate to go through with them. It's why the best part of delivering a presentation is preparing the slides. I'm a creator. What about you?

TAKE ACTION

- → Knowing that there isn't only one right way to achieve your goal, how would you do it in a way that is effortless for you?
- → If you were to look at your own work and hobbies, are you a creator or a performer? How can you do more of what feels in alignment with who you are?

THOUGHTS TO PRACTISE

- → There is always a way that feels good.
- → It's OK to do what's effortless.

PART 2
EMOTIONAL ENERGY

I've said it before, and I'll say it again: I love thinking. I love spending time inside my mind generating ideas, refining them, prepping, planning, rehearsing, making decisions, creating the future and imagining extraordinary possibilities. There are many times when I come back from a daydreaming session with words ready to be set on the page already edited, with commitments to new projects or goals and ideas that are already shaped and meticulously planned. From the outside, it might seem like I just came up with them. But on the inside, a long, detailed process took place, invisible to the rest of the world. It feels like living in a parallel reality.

This is a superpower, one that I encourage you to use to your advantage. However, there's always the other side of the coin. Just as you can spend time thinking about positive outcomes and using that mental energy to focus on what you want to create, you can spend time imagining negative scenarios and draining your brain power on what you want to avoid creating. There's only so much mental energy you can generate every day, and when you spend too much of it on negatives, there's not much left to use for the positives.

That's not all that your thoughts do though. They also create emotion, and emotion is what makes you take action or avoid taking action. Thoughts are essentially the first step of creation, and you can learn to control them in order to feel your way into a better life. Don't worry, I'll explain this in detail later.

This section of the book will help you understand your feelings, process them and, when possible, change them. We'll also explore the most common emotions that might hold you back – worry, rejection, stress, fear of failure, fear or success, fear of discomfort, and fear of what other people will think of you – and find either ways to reframe the situation or solutions to cope. I'll also give you some ideas on how to make quicker decisions in order to avoid confusion and overwhelm, and some more tools to help your over-thinking brain.

Chapter 6
Emotional intelligence

Imagine this: what if you could easily handle any emotion? What would you be able to do? That's right: anything.

Before we go back to strategies, let's stop and talk about our feelings. Wow, I bet you never expected an introvert to say that. But don't worry, I don't mean it 'that way'. You won't have to share anything, though I might. You already know a lot about me, so I might as well continue.

Emotions are important because how you feel will be one of the main stoppers when it comes to networking, public speaking or even taking on challenging work. The fear of discomfort, disappointment or rejection can be a lot more powerful than the desire to achieve a new goal. But imagine this: what if you could easily handle absolutely any emotion? What would you be able to do? That's right: anything.

In this chapter, we'll look at a few different ways to deal with difficult emotions; but before we start... what are emotions? From a technical point of view, your feelings are effects of the mix of chemicals your body releases during an event. It's a cocktail of hormones, neurotransmitters, electrical impulses and fluids running through the body producing sensations. Some of them are automated responses of the body to certain events, created through repetition and experience. Others are produced by the thoughts you're thinking – consciously or not – and a change of thought will result in a change of feeling too.

Question and change the rules

What drains us emotionally is dwelling on negative feelings like worry, anxiety, guilt, stress or overwhelm as a learned response. I noticed that I, and many others, had learned what the appropriate reaction to events 'should' be – like an unwritten manual of human emotional behaviour that we follow without questioning. This is how it is. If you have a lot to do, you feel stressed. If there's uncertainty, you feel anxious. If you lose your job, you feel worried and sad. If your child breaks a glass, you feel angry.

These learned reactions create a default response to life, and you're very rarely told that you can choose how you feel about anything. You are told sometimes that you can change how you process a certain emotion, for example going for a walk instead of punching the wall when you're angry, but not that you can feel a different emotion altogether. While that is still great advice, and we will cover some of it too, it leaves out the possibility of making yourself feel better by neither hurting yourself nor having to leave the house to walk a few anger-releasing miles.

Some introverts tend to not process emotions at all. We push them away, pretend they're not there or feel ashamed or fearful of them. Hands up if while growing up you were told that some of your emotions are silly, that it's shameful to cry, that you need to 'man up' or repress some emotions because they're embarrassing. Some of us were also overprotected by our parents, and I can understand how we'd like to see our children being happy all the time. While it has usually come from a positive and loving place, this has created a world where adults are incapable of handling negative emotions. We drink, eat and work our asses off to avoid feelings.

But feeling and understanding emotion can be an asset, albeit uncom-fortable at times. Negative feelings can give you an insight into what you want to create, have or change in life. They can also show you that what you're thinking in that moment is causing you pain, and you have an opportunity to change it. You always have a choice. You can choose to not feel stressed, overwhelmed, disappointed, worried, angry, no matter what happens to you. You can set the intention of what your response will be to every event, interaction, task or problem you need to solve. Right now, decide that you're going to question everything that you accepted as truth when it comes to how to feel, and allow yourself to write your own book of rules.

If you watch the behaviour of successful people, you'll understand why this is important. They are able to go through failures, handle high-pressure moments, make tough decisions quickly or tackle high amounts of tasks without mentally breaking down, which would happen to someone with less emotional intelligence. They achieve this by thinking differently and processing feelings differently.

When you can change how you feel

Think about a lemon. Imagine you pick up a knife and cut it in half. Then, imagine you cut one juicy slice and bring it to your mouth. See and feel the lemon as vividly as you can. What just happened? If your mouth is watering, it's to be expected.

Now move on to imagine a busy coffee shop with jazz music in the background along with the buzz of people working on their computers and staff bringing drinks or clearing tables. If you feel motivated and inspired to go and work too, that's to be expected.

And lastly, think about something that makes you happy. And if this is a good time in your day for a one-minute break, close your eyes and really allow yourself to process that image. How do you feel?

All these examples are here to show you what feelings are – sensations in the body produced by the brain while you think about people, places or events. The lemon wasn't real. The coffee shop wasn't real. The memory, while of a real event, wasn't happening right now. It wasn't the existence or reality of the event that produced the feeling; it was the fact that you thought about it. Actually, the brain doesn't even know the difference between reality and imagination, and thoughts are neither good nor bad, true nor false, but neutral sentences that travel through the mind.

When you think, your brain produces a combination of chemicals that starts to travel through your body, creating sensations. For example, if you think about something that you're afraid of or remember a thriller movie scene that made an impression on you, your brain will order the production of adrenaline. Along with adrenaline that will travel very fast, the heart will start beating faster, and you will feel the sensations you associate with fear.

Let's imagine you have parents with a bad habit of commenting what a mess your apartment is every time they visit. It's happened so many times that now just the thought of them visiting makes you angry in advance. You expect them to say what they always say, and yourself to feel how you always feel. But where did the anger come from in the first place? From the thought you first had when you were told you didn't do a great job clearing out the mess.

Maybe it was 'They never approve of anything!', 'They always manage to find something wrong' or 'This is my house, what gives them the right?' You can easily associate these thoughts with anger or something similar. But what if the thoughts could have been: 'I know this is how they are – I'll nod and move on', 'Hmmm, that's right, I could probably give the windows a quick wipe too' or 'I think it's clean enough and I'm happy with the result'? These will change the feeling to something like calm with a hint of disappointment, but without the tightness of anger or frustration. It's a lot more neutral than anything from the first list.

Once you can see how a change in thoughts can change the emotion you feel, you can choose the feelings you want to shift and start to plan better interpretations. However, knowing that some of your responses are now automatic, you need to set the intention ahead of the event so you can practise in your mind how you want to react. In the example above, you'd simply tell yourself that it's OK for your parents to have their own opinions, but you want to stop feeling angry every time they visit. This cannot continue until the end of time. You decide to feel calm whatever they say, and even though your own habits of feeling angry might kick in, you'll remind yourself of the new intention to interrupt the pattern and practise some of the positive thoughts listed above. If this is hard to do in your mind in the beginning, you can set up phone alarms at appropriate times with the positive thoughts or even wear a bracelet or piece of clothing to regularly remind you to check in with yourself and change your state if necessary.

To sum it up in a process to remember, these are the steps:

1. Set your intention for the new emotion. (E.g. 'I want to feel calm instead of angry.')
2. Brainstorm some thoughts that can create that emotion. What's true enough for you to believe and will create a better experience for you? (E.g. 'I know they will comment again – they do it all the time. They are entitled to their own opinions and so am I.')
3. Practise the thoughts in your mind ahead of the event.
4. Expect to want to feel your habitual feelings. It's human nature.
5. As the event happens, check your feelings regularly. Interrupt the pattern as many times as it's needed by switching to your new thoughts. Use a phone alarm or any other type of physical reminder if that makes it easier to remember.

If there's something that has great potential for stressing me out, it has to be going to the Romanian Embassy to renew my passport. I know there's going to be a queue; I know people are loud and agitated; I know the building is far away and not easily accessible by public transport. It's the perfect recipe for me to spend a whole day affected by negative energy, and that used to be the case before I understood I can absolutely change that. As I plan my trip and on the day of the visit, I tell myself the following thoughts:

➔ 'No matter how the others behave, I can stay calm.'
➔ 'Everyone here has their own problems – I can choose to feel compassionate.'

➔ 'I have the whole day for this, so it doesn't matter how long the queue is.'
➔ 'Other people's emotions are not mine to borrow.'
➔ 'It's all for a greater purpose – I get to travel.'

As I open the door at the embassy, I take a deep breath and again I repeat these in my mind. They keep me grounded and calm in a moment when I could easily become impatient and irritated like most of my fellow Romanians looking to sort out their travel paperwork.

Knowing that it's your thoughts that cause your emotions gives you both a lot of power and a lot of responsibility. Knowing that no one else is capable of making you happy, stressed or angry puts you in the driver's seat. Not only you can shift those feelings, but you are also allowed to. Just because you learned to respond in a certain way doesn't make it the right way. It's not only OK to question your current habits, it's highly recommended.

You can apply this to your entire life and to each and every interaction you have. You probably already know the situations that tend to always trigger the same emotion. What are those? What's the emotion? How do you want to feel instead? What can you think differently in order to feel the new emotion? What are some problems at work you could look at differently? Who are the people who you thought were making you feel a certain emotion and how can you take that responsibility back?

Reframing the past

Sometimes I wish I had had this information years ago. I would go back in time and suffer a lot less. I might still have taken the same actions, but the experiences would have felt less negative.

I moved to London because I was frustrated with my job back home. I was passed over for a promotion three times, and eventually lost my patience and left. I was full of hate and blamed everyone else for how I was feeling, for how much money I was making, for how much I worked, and I spent most of my days dwelling in anger and resentment. This is what I was thinking then:

'That guy only got the promotion because he goes out to lunch with the manager.'

'I only get the less interesting projects.'

'I spend my whole life working for others and I can't even afford the rent on my own.'

'Why isn't anything changing?'

I picked this example because unhappiness at work is common. We almost expect to feel frustrated, to complain about money, complain about the boss, and generally add drama and fall into victimisation. It's what we do. If I were to go back in time and change my situation, I would take radical responsibility for my life and stop blaming others for my results. No one forced me to work as much. Really.

I still believe some of those old thoughts were true. I absolutely deserved that promotion and a lot more money than I was earning, and I still don't remember some people with fondness; my feelings for them are neutral at best. But I also believe that everyone did the best they knew how to; they didn't learn otherwise. I didn't yet know enough to change anything. I was overworked, but I also acquired a lot of skills that helped me later.

And what a blessing it was to not be promoted! What if I had been and I had stayed? I would have missed the whole of the rest of my life, including the move to London and everything that it brought. Most of my growth happened because I got fed up and left. However, I could have reached the same conclusion without the extra suffering my thoughts added. I could have left *happy*. I don't expect myself to have had the wisdom I have now – I was only 24 after all. But a few small shifts would have helped a lot. What if I had thought...

'Even if I get the promotion or not, I'm doing all this work for myself and my development.'

'I would do it differently, but to each their own.'

'I'm responsible for my success, so I'll do the best I can. But all I can do is all I can do.'

'How can I be an example for my team?'

'What else could I read or learn to try to make some changes?'

'How could I help others improve?'

You can sense the shift in energy: from the resentful victim to the empowered and resilient woman taking charge of her destiny and making the most of an unfortunate situation. The change in attitude wouldn't have meant a change in results, as most of the decisions were made by other people and involved a lot more details than just my own performance, but my experience would have changed. Maybe I would have enjoyed life more. Maybe I would have cried less. Maybe I would have taken even more responsibilities.

Who knows?

But even reframing it now has had a positive impact on me. I have been able to let go of the resentment and even be grateful for the life I created for myself later on.

What past event could you rewrite to let go of hard feelings? Being cheated on? Being lied to? Losing a job? Missing an opportunity? Why was it a blessing? What have you learned? What did it make possible for you?

Shame and guilt are two common feelings that are connected to the past and can easily be dropped with a change in thinking. Just as with forgiving other people and understanding that how they acted was the best they knew, so you can forgive yourself. You always do the best you can. You always act according to the amount of knowledge and wisdom you have in that moment. All kids behave the same. All teenagers behave the same. All 24-year-olds behave the same. There is no point in expecting myself from 15 years ago to have the same mindset I have today.

However, you won't always manage to put a positive spin on a situation. It would be weird to laugh at a funeral or when your manager tells you that you're fired. You don't have to always find the lesson, the blessing or the better feeling interpretation.

Sometimes you'll feel sad, disappointed, angry or frustrated and that's OK. What you need to do instead of reframing the situation is to handle the emotion with calm and grace because punching a co-worker or smashing your computer is frowned upon.

Preparing for rejection

Just like the Oscar nominees, you need to be prepared with both a winning speech and a loser's smile. I once coached an introvert through getting a promotion. Apart from strategically planning all her steps and interactions, including the wording for emails or mentoring juniors, she also prepared for the meeting in which her manager delivered the result of that round of reviews. How would you respond to a yes? But most importantly, how would you respond to a no? Here's how she went into the meeting. The thoughts she practised to keep her calm no matter the result were:

'I did my best according to the requirements of the promotion. I learned a lot, made important connections and delivered high-quality work.'

'I know there are a lot more aspects involved in who's rewarded apart from my individual performance.'

'Whatever the decision, my manager is merely the messenger.'

'I want my reaction to be worthy of someone who would have got the promotion. I will behave as the leader I am, even if the title is not going to be delivered to me right now.'

'I have nothing to prove to anyone.'

'My co-workers know my value and appreciate my work.'

The practised response to a yes was: 'That's great, thank you! Do you have any feedback I could take on?' The practised response to a no was: 'That's a shame. Do you have any feedback I could take on, and next steps to prepare for the next round?'

The day came and her manager told a lot of people no, including her. The response was the one we rehearsed together, and, as her manager later told her, it was an impressively calm reaction considering the circumstances. Of course she was disappointed and she didn't hide this. But disappointment doesn't have to look like a drama scene. No need for tears, throwing objects or smashing the virtual door behind you by exiting the Zoom meeting without saying goodbye.

Feelings are to be felt; all the actions you take while the emotion is present are re-actions. They are responses to the feeling, not the feeling itself. The feeling is internal and can be invisible if you want it to, reactions being what other people see. You can still say 'I'm disappointed' and look like you are, without reacting like some of my client's colleagues actually did – from throwing tantrums all the way to quitting their jobs (yep, just like me).

Whether you know it or not, people are watching you. Not long after my client decided to graciously take the no but keep behaving like the leader she wanted to be, she was approached by another team and offered a new role inside the same company – a leading role better than the one she had her eyes on. On her career path, this new role would have been the next step after the promotion, but her efforts were rewarded ahead of time. This was an even better result than the one we worked together for, and it was a combination of good strategy and increased emotional intelligence.

Throughout your journey to greatness, being told no will be one of the biggest challenges. You should always be prepared to get the Oscar, but also to clap and nod for the winners when you don't. Often, being told no has nothing to do with you or your performance. Take the lesson you need from the experience and then move on until you get a yes.

This is one of the tough training lessons all entrepreneurs need to go through, which makes us eventually immune to rejection. But the more nos, the more yeses. The bigger the nos, the better the yeses. As a business owner, if I make a pitch to 100 people, statistically only 20 of them will say yes. Which means that I will get 80 nos. But I can't get the 20 yeses without the 80 nos. What started off as painful is now just a numbers game. Are you willing to honour the statistics and keep trying until you get to the yes?

Rejection is not personal. No one is saying no to you as a human. They're saying no to an idea you produced that's not right for them at the moment, or no to giving you more money or a different role because there isn't enough money to give out. When it's a lack of skill, take the feedback and get better. When it's bad timing, come back later. When there's nothing you can do about it... Oh, well...

Processing emotion

Sometimes you won't want to choose a different thought to feel a different feeling. In some cases, you won't be able to. You'll have to feel fear, anxiety, disappointment, and do it without negative consequences. You can choose a better reaction to all your emotions, or, as mentioned, no reaction at all. This is a lot different to not feeling the emotion though. You're not trying to push it away, but to process it internally by bringing your awareness to the sensations of the body and breathing them out.

To do this, I have a four-step process I use for a whole range of emotions, including anxiety, grief and even one that might not be perceived as a feeling: food cravings. It's easy to remember by thinking about the names of the steps: 'Stop and say your ABC.'

1. **Stop**. When you catch yourself feeling the emotion, stop yourself from taking any action.
2. **A**wareness. What are you feeling? Become present with the emotion, recognise it and analyse it. 'I'm feeling fear. My lips are buzzing. My heart is racing.'
3. **B**reath. Take six deep breaths, in through the nose and out through the mouth. As you do so while feeling the emotion, the intensity will decrease.
4. **C**hoice. Do you want to take any action now that you're calmer?

Feelings are not dangerous. You are capable of handling every single one of them, including anger, sadness, disappointment, frustration, anxiety or embarrassment. Everything you do or don't do is because you feel a certain way, you want to feel a certain way or you want to avoid feeling a certain way; for example, you won't ask for a raise because you're afraid you're going to be rejected. But what if the feeling wouldn't be a big deal?

When you know you can feel anything, everything becomes possible. And this is the best thing about emotions: they work like antibiotics – the more you feel them, the less effective they are. If embarrassment became an emotion that didn't scare you anymore, what would you do? If fear was easy to feel, what would you have the courage to start?

TAKE ACTION

Practise feeling your feelings right now, so you can use this during a negative experience. Close your eyes and focus on the sensations of your body. If you find it difficult, try a guided mindfulness meditation, as it uses the same principles and can be a great starting point.

THOUGHTS TO PRACTISE

→ I am capable of feeling anything. Feelings are harmless.
→ My feelings are caused by my thoughts, not by events or people. I can change them if I want to.
→ All my emotions are valid. I am allowed to feel them.
→ I have the right to change all my learned responses to events so I can feel better.
→ Rejection is not about me.

Chapter 7
Stop the worry

---

*You can make yourself sick by thinking,
or you can make yourself happy,
healthy and successful.*

My mind never takes a break. I'm constantly creating another world in my mind, thinking about all the possible scenarios, worrying about everything from whether I can pay my taxes to climate change and how the world is doomed. Being in the present moment has always been a challenge because my thoughts take me away from the now and into an imagined life that may or may not be manifested.

I've always been a worrier. Of course, the younger I was, the smaller the worry. It started as overthinking about not doing well in art class and the impending low grade I'd get; it increased to having to repay a loan to my roommate in college when I had obviously spent everything; it got all the way to right now… worrying about whether my dogs will get cancer, spending hours of thinking time on how I put on a pound, or that earless dog I saw on the PETA website a few years ago. If you ever thought that in a contest of the most ridiculous worry you'd win, we obviously haven't met before. I'd crush it.

On the flip side, isn't it wonderful when you overthink about the possible positive outcomes, reaching your goals or what life would look like if you lived on an island and worked when and how you wanted? This is the kind of daydreaming we love, and it's produced by the exact same brain that imagines the deaths of loved ones and homelessness. It's great to know that it's capable of both because when you catch yourself thinking about the bad, you can redirect your thoughts to the good.

Thinking takes a lot of energy, 30 per cent of your daily energy expenditure being attributed to the brain. Isn't it a waste if most of that goes towards making you miserable? When worry takes over and becomes your default state, in time it can lead to anxiety, depression, OCD, burnout or physical pain. You can make yourself sick by thinking, or you can make yourself happy, healthy and successful.

Of course, not worrying anymore is a lot easier to think about than to do. I'm sure you had your fair share of well-intended friends telling you 'It's going to be fine!' and 'Don't worry about it'. Yeah, like that hasn't crossed my mind. But that was never good enough. You don't let it go only because someone considers you can figure it out. You only let it go once you have spent a good few days/ weeks/months pondering and you decide that it's finally settled.

It has happened to me more than once that when I vocalised my worry to a friend, they tried to encourage me that it's going to be fine. I said OK but kept thinking about it for weeks, and then I brought it up again in a month still 100 per cent fresh from my mind. They barely remembered what I was talking about. 'What? You're still thinking about that?' 'Yes, yes I am. I thought about it for the last 27 days because that's how my brain works, and I hate that you don't understand that.'

Sometimes talking to a friend about a worry helps immensely. It can be reassuring to know that something you consider of extreme importance and potentially life altering is a lot smaller from another point of view. You get relief – at least for a while because there's a big chance that wasn't good enough for your brain and some more ruminating needs to happen. But the core problem is your thinking, and that's where the solution needs to come from too.

Why we worry

In the book *The Worry Cure*, Dr Robert L. Leahy (2006) talks about all the reasons why we worry and what we can do about it. I've picked some of the most relevant ones for us and added my own interpretation and advice, but if you want a deep dive into this emotion, *The Worry Cure* is an insightful book.

Worrying gives you a sense of control

What your mind is looking for when you're worrying is certainty. It needs to be sure you know all the possible outcomes and have solutions for them if they're not the intended one. You want to know and be sure of everything. This would work if your brain thought it was good enough. Just like the 'It's gonna be fine' reassurance, it gives you temporary relief. Whenever I used to worry about money, I created a budget and that offered me as much certainty as I could get.

But it doesn't end here. As time passes and things evolve, so do your worries. There are now more scenarios, more possibilities, and considering all of them can be a never-ending process. Looking for certainty will never be a one-time action; it's a continuous practice, and it's knowing this that gives you a choice: worry forever or let go of control.

You'll never get to be 100 per cent certain 100 per cent of the time, but you can get to a level that gives you enough mental energy and space to move from worry to calm. As in my budgeting example, you can make enough changes in your environment or in your routine to give you a sense of knowing that can settle your brain for a while. You can go down the rabbit hole and consider a bunch of scenarios and have plans for them. But then you'll have to decide that this is enough, at least for now, and redirect your mind to positives whenever you catch yourself worrying. This has to become a habit that will need your full awareness and time to change. In the chapter that follows, I'll give you examples of what this can look like.

You're designed this way

Certainty also means safety. As humans, we're primed to constantly look out for the dangers in our environments so we can run, hide or fight. It's how we evolved, though the dangers that used to loom over our ancestors are long gone. Knowing that this is normal behaviour can be very helpful in reducing some of the guilt and general bad feeling that comes with worry.

You think it's the responsible thing to do

What if you let go of those terrible thoughts and you lose control of the situation? Doesn't worrying mean you care? But imagining terrible scenarios doesn't make you more responsible or more likely to succeed; you can still show you care even if you don't worry constantly. What if you focused on what can go right and put your energy there instead?

I love this quote from Dr Joe Dispenza (2014) that says 'where you place your focus is where you place your energy'. It makes it obvious that when we obsess about everything that can go wrong, we can accidentally make it happen. When all you can see in your mind is one specific result, your thoughts, your emotions and your actions will follow it. We call them self-fulfilling prophecies, but they are in fact, logical outcomes.

You probably understand this for a positive outcome. Let's say you want to get a new job. All you think about is getting a new job. You start to get excited. You look for jobs. You apply. And boom! New job! It all started with a thought. But what if it's negative? If all you can think about is 'I hope I don't get fired', your general feeling will be fear. You become it. You act out of fear. You're sloppy and keep hiding. You don't take bold action and never make yourself seen. The review time comes. Verdict: you did a really bad job. Result: you get fired. It all starts with a thought. The responsible thing to do is make it positive.

You might think it works

'I worried before and those terrible outcomes didn't happen. This must mean it worked.' No, it didn't. Most of the things we worry about simply don't happen. It's a case of statistics more than causality. You might believe it's because you were prepared for them. Would they have happened if you didn't? The truth is probably somewhere in the middle. However, no matter how much you prepare, life has the ability to throw you some curveballs, and it's almost never what you worried about. When it happens, I can guarantee you'll manage it. You've been doing that your whole life.

Letting go of worry

Letting go of worry is not easy. I really, really believe you. Someone saying 'Stop thinking about it, it's all going to be fine' doesn't work, even when that someone is you. While stopping completely is impossible to do immediately, there are ways to contain your emotions and process the thoughts creating them.

Journaling

Give yourself ten minutes of 'worry time' every day. Pick up a journal and write for that whole time, complaining and worrying about everything you want. Doing that will help you feel better in the moment but will also give you the opportunity to look back at your thoughts and call out some of those lying bastards. When you see your mind on paper, you see both what's true and what's not. Keeping it all in your head will make all of it seem honest and urgent. Once exposed though, you can see that 'My family will stop helping me', 'I will die homeless and alone' or 'No one will buy my book' are awful lies and terrible things to say to yourself. I mean, come on, at least my mum and my brother will buy the damn book.

Knowing this will give you another superpower – talking back to yourself. During the day, after worry time is over, you'll naturally think some worry thoughts – it's a habit. But now you can stop believing them and talk back, interrupting the pattern by simply saying: 'Stop. Not true.' And when you stop the thought, you stop the feeling too.

Talk to a coach or a therapist

Regular sessions with a professional 'listener' can help you find calm and grounding, but also develop better beliefs and coping mechanisms. In some cases, simply voicing your worries will help you realise that the words coming out of your mouth are crazy talk. In some other cases, the coach will be the one to point out that what you're considering a fact is indeed an opinion, and she'll help you reframe it or offer an alternative thought to think that feels better.

TAKE ACTION

Take ten minutes for the worry time journaling exercise. Once you're done, we can move on to look at some specific cases of worries we love to torment ourselves with in the following chapters.

THOUGHTS TO PRACTISE

→ I care even if I don't worry.
→ I'm responsible even if I don't worry.
→ The responsible thing to do is to focus on the positives.
→ Worrying is a completely natural thing. There's nothing wrong with me.
→ Thank you, brain! I know you're trying to protect me, but I've got this.

Chapter 8
The fear of failure:
what if it doesn't work?

Failure is always an opinion, not a truth.

I haven't met anyone so far who was, by default, happy to fail. We're conditioned to avoid being wrong. Maybe it's the way we were brought up. Our parents had high expectations. We had to get good grades, behave all the time and never break anything. Otherwise, they said, there would be consequences.

I feared the 'consequences' so much, I never got to learn what they were. I once got a bad grade in maths and even though I didn't mind, I knew my parents would. I wasn't ready to face what was on the other side of a failure, so I pretended I cared. I went home and put on the most repentant face I could; I also cried a lot. They felt bad for me, so they skipped the punishment, if ever there was any. I didn't get in trouble that day but I also never got another bad grade; even more, I became one of the best at maths in the county, representing my school in multiple competitions.

We fear consequences. But what are those? What's the result of a failed interview? Or of a failed business? Or bankruptcy? Or divorce? What is so bad about them that we'd rather stay away from even trying? It feels like the worst that can happen is death. But is that true?

The rabbit hole

The rabbit hole is the exercise I go through every time I'm afraid of a negative outcome. It starts with a simple question: what's the worst that can happen?

Example one:

What's the worst that can happen if you go to an interview for a job you'd like?

They won't like you.

And what's the worst that can happen?

They'll reject your application.

And what's the worst that can happen?

You'll feel rejected and won't get the job.

In this example, the worst thing that can happen is feeling rejected. Feelings, as we already discussed, are harmless and you're capable of experiencing all of them. Another negative result of this scenario is not getting the job, but that's also the case if you don't go to the interview at all. Going to the interview increases your chances though.

Example two:

What's the worst that can happen if you quit your job to start a business?

The business won't work and you'll use all your savings.

Then what's the worst that can happen?

You have to sell your home and live somewhere else for a while.

Then what's the worst that can happen?

Business is still not working and you have to move in with your parents.

Then what's the worst that can happen?

They throw you out and you'll be homeless. You will probably feel rejected, unloved and unsuccessful.

Example two shows us that you can go deep down the rabbit hole, and that you can take different actions at each step. You can always change course and the worst thing that can happen is very unlikely and a long way ahead. I also want to point out that it's not the actual results that you would fear, but how those results would feel. With increased emotional intelligence, this will no longer be an issue.

What is failure anyway?

Failure is always an opinion, not a truth. What you might consider failure, someone else might see as neutral. Do you believe killing a plant is a failure? I don't, but a gardener might. What about a book that only sold a few copies? The author might call it a failure, but someone who's waiting on the sidelines to write one will call it a success and admire the courage to hit 'publish' or to even get started in the first place. Changing your interpretation of the results of your actions is always the quickest way to change how you feel about them.

Failure is necessary information; it tells you what doesn't work. You can make nothing of it and try something new. Life is full of tiny failures anyway, but we choose to ignore them. OK, I admit, I'm sometimes disappointed if I cook a bad meal or write a bad email, but once I've accepted that those are part of the learning process, I can look at what went wrong in a spirit of curiosity. Was it too much salt? Did I overcook the lentils (again)?

Is it the size of the failure that makes us care or not? Though it might be true in some cases, even the day-to-day failures can hurt if we make them mean something about us, and if, in some way, they relate to our identity. My lentil bolognese might not be a big deal for me, but it would be for someone who considers themselves a cook.

However, it's not possible to never make mistakes. Accepting that some days you'll overcook the lentils, accidentally buy the wrong type of tomato sauce or send an email to the wrong list means accepting you're human. And humans are not perfect, even on their best days.

But, what's even more important is that the outcome is not You. The project you want to start is not you. The book you want to write is not you. Whether the book sells zero copies or a million doesn't say anything about you. Your work is an extension of you, but is not who you are. It's a product of your ideas and your skills in a particular moment.

When you change your relationship with failure, life suddenly has more potential to be fulfilling, and, why not, extraordinary. You allow yourself to try new experiences and set bigger goals without the fear of the outcome. Obstacles along the way are normal though sometimes they're unexpected; how you respond to them will decide whether the experience is a failure or not. Think about it this way: if you continue to move on and jump through every hoop, you'll never fail; you'll either succeed or try again.

When you go to a new place for the very first time, you input the address into your GPS and start the journey. However, if you encounter an accident, you might have to pause for a while or change the route. Then you're slowed down by traffic. Then you notice your motorway exit has just been closed. But do you ever consider not getting to your destination at all? Maybe on that first day you decide to turn around and try again tomorrow. But you know you will eventually find the location. The accident and the traffic are never part of the plan, though you always know they might happen. You don't let them be reasons to stop. On that day though, that just wasn't the path to the goal.

Before I became successful in business, I launched plenty of products and tried multiple ideas. Some worked well, some had moderate success, but many of them were complete failures. For every single one of those, I kept telling myself that it wasn't supposed to work; it was supposed to teach me a lesson. And they do. Failures teach you what doesn't work, so you can make space in your life and mind to create something else. Something that can be successful. And the quicker you fail, the quicker you can move on.

Every single new try develops your character, teaches you new skills and gives you more experience. Once I had the business that worked, all those that didn't work finally made sense. They got me ready for the big break, 'seasoned' me and helped me discover who I really am in this area of my life. As Bill Gates says in a famous quote from *The Road Ahead*, 'Success is a lousy teacher.' When you achieve your goal from the very first try, you miss out on the opportunity to become the 'fail detective', to evaluate every step and every result along the way, and then see all the possibilities for improvements.

You also skip the feeling of accomplishment and pride that you get when you see the growth from one iteration to another. If you're a runner, you know how it feels to achieve a new personal best after trying to break it several times to no avail. How boring would life be if there were no setbacks? How boring would games be if you won every single time?

Though I'm encouraging you to fail more, I won't lie to you; it doesn't feel very nice. The intensity of the emotion increases with the size of the failure, from the disappointment of a tiny mistake to the deep pain of an absolute flop. But that pain, as bitter as it is, is only a feeling, and feelings don't kill. (Unless you believe in dying from a broken heart.)

Emotions are harmless and, thankfully, they lose their power even more as you experience them. Because of the chemical nature, to produce the same intensity every time, your experience needs to be more intense too. This means that once you allow yourself to feel disappointed once, you'll feel it a lot less in a future situation. Running away from pain is in your DNA, but most of today's pain is emotional. Teach your brain that it's OK to feel the effects of failure and you'll open the door to a world of possibilities. When you're not afraid of feelings such as disappointment, sadness, embarrass-ment or frustration, there is nothing that can stop you from getting to the finish line. The good news is, once you have done it once, it gets much easier.

TAKE ACTION

Go down the rabbit hole. What's the worst that can happen if you start working towards your goal?

THOUGHTS TO PRACTISE

➔ Failure is an interpretation, not a truth.
➔ The worst that can happen is an unpleasant feeling, and I am capable of feeling anything.
➔ I am not my creation, be it good or bad.
➔ The quicker I fail, the quicker I can move on.
➔ I'll either succeed or try again.
➔ Failure is only information.

Chapter 9
The fear of success:
what if it works and it's terrible?

'If I get rich, my friends won't talk to me
anymore,' said your brain
subconsciously...

'How's that big project coming along? Did you present it to your manager?' I asked, having been told about the idea and thought it was really good. A promotion for my client would have been very likely if this project happened.

'Not yet, I didn't have time,' she responded, knowing that I'm not going to believe that.

'Do you want the project to be successful? Do you want it to happen?' I continued, hoping for a loose thread I could pull.

'I do, but it's so big...'

'So? What's the problem with that?'

'What if I have to travel a lot, be away from home or be in meetings all day long?'

'What if? Would that be worth it?'

'I don't want that to happen, no.'

'Can you be in that position without being away from home or in meetings all day? Would you have the option to adapt the job to your needs? Or… not do it? You know, no one will force you to get promoted. But if you believe in this project, you can do it anyway.'

It's been two years since this discussion with my coaching client. Though she believed in the project and could see the impact it could have on the entire organisation, she was always coming up with excuses for not creating a proposal, lack of time being the most common one. I wanted to understand where her procrastination was coming from, since I know she's an action taker and top performer in all areas. As I'm typing this, the project hasn't happened, but that's because the circumstances have changed, not because the fear of negative outcomes was stronger than the joy of the positives.

Though less intuitive than the fear of failure, the fear of success kills as many dreams as its more famous cousin. They do have one thing in common: they're mostly unconscious. You never intentionally think about the new responsibilities that come with a promotion, or that your friends might not like you anymore if you get rich, or that if the business becomes a success, you'll have to hire people and that's way outside of your comfort zone. But the thoughts are there, hidden in your mind, sabotaging you and holding you back from even taking the first step. Here are a few more examples.

If I get rich:

➔ … my friends won't talk to me anymore
➔ … I won't have any real friends because everyone will be after my money
➔ … my children will grow up with too many privileges
➔ … I'll have to pay more taxes and there is a lot of paperwork
➔ … life will be more stressful.

If my book gets published:

➔ … people will find out about me and might reach out
➔ … I'll have to go on a book tour or host launches.

If I sell an online course:

➔ … I'll get mean replies from unhappy students
➔ … I will have the responsibility to deliver on time on what I promised

→ ... I will have to make sure students go through the course and have results

→ ... my friends will laugh at me, saying it's not a real business.

If I start dating again:

→ ... I will have less time for myself

→ ... my job performance will drop.

If I get promoted:

→ ... I'll have less flexibility

→ ... I'll have more meetings and travel more

→ ... I won't have time for my hobbies anymore.

You might be laughing at some of these. Maybe because you think they're silly, or maybe because you believe them too.

When I created my first ever online course, I went through this exercise, asking myself what's the worst that could happen if I created and sold it, and people bought it. I was afraid of the responsibility that would come with bringing it out into the world. People would follow my advice and get or not get results. What if they didn't? When the first buyer signed up, the course was still in progress and knowing I couldn't back out was scary too. What if something happened and I couldn't deliver?

Well... here's how that went down. I delivered ahead of time, but not the course. Something I haven't mentioned yet was that I was seven months pregnant when I started working on this product. I thought I had plenty of time to complete it. But about three weeks into the process, with plenty of lessons already available for my students but the course not even close to the finish line, my little one decided that it was time to join us. Six weeks ahead of the due date. To say that I wasn't ready would be an understatement. The house wasn't ready, I had no hospital bag, I hadn't planned my maternity leave yet, projects were far from being completed, and I had these people who had bought from me expecting me to show up and help them.

My biggest fear was now a reality and I had to deal with it. With labour lasting for about 20 hours while I was on my own in the hospital due to the pandemic restrictions, I had time. I texted everyone enrolled in the course in between contractions. I knew life was about to change. Even with my usual energy and eagerness, this was different. I had to accept that sleepless nights and exhaustion were coming, and even if it's hard to admit, I'm not superhuman.

Baby P was born in June; I finally completed the course in October. Everyone was understanding and didn't let one very special circumstance change their opinion about who I am as a human, as a teacher or a business owner. Though what I had feared eventually happened, I handled it as best as I could. And so can you.

Once you're aware of what scares you, you are able to plan better. You can choose not to go ahead; sometimes the negative consequences outweigh the positives, and you shouldn't feel pressured to make a decision that will make your life miserable. However, many times you'll decide to move forward and find solutions to possible problems before they arise. Or, if the solution is not obvious yet, you can at least trust in your ability to figure it out in the moment. 'Cross that bridge when you get to it,' as they say.

When you bring your fears out in the open, they become less powerful and you have the upper hand. With everything down on paper, possible obstacles become strategies. And with a solid plan, you can finally move your idea from dream to goal.

TAKE ACTION

Take 15 minutes to write: what's the worst that can happen if your idea becomes a success?

THOUGHTS TO PRACTISE

→ Not everything I think is true.
→ I trust that I'll find solutions to my problems.

Chapter 10
The fear of discomfort: what if it's going to be hard?

Life right now, good or bad, is only comfortable because it's what you know, even if it's not good for you; even if it's painful, it's a pain you're already familiar with.

I'm not going to lie about this one. It will probably be hard. If it wasn't, you would have done it by now, as with any other small tasks on your to-do list. But goals are not to-do lists; they come with challenges. Whether it's true or not that it's going to be hard is not even relevant. What matters is that thinking of it like that doesn't help. Instead, it puts a huge STOP sign in front of the start line. You haven't even taken the first step and you're already pulling back. It's understandable; it can be overwhelming, especially if you've attempted it before and your experience is telling you it's going to be very uncomfortable.

But what is the discomfort anyway? Usually, an unpleasant emotion. And you already know everything you need to know about emotions. All you need to do is take the first step and get the ball rolling. However, in this case, the procrastination comes from focusing on the pain instead of the growth. Discomfort is inevitable;

you experience it almost every day. But there is something special about this one: it's self-inflicted and leads to progress.

There's something weirdly pleasant about committing to being uncomfortable for the sake of achieving a big goal. It gives you a sense of pride, accomplishment and even superiority. You're able to handle the pain for a very long time and you know most people can't. But you are not most people. You're extraordinary.

If we consider the example of weight loss, what most people think about first are the foods they're going to miss out on, the excruciatingly painful workouts and the soreness that follows, the sugar cravings and all the times they gave in before, all the past diets that worked or not, the calorie counting that apart from becoming an unhealthy obsession is a new habit that needs time to be built, and so on.

Who would be excited to get started while thinking about all these? No matter how badly you want the result, knowing it takes getting through months or sometimes years of pain can make even the most committed person give up. As clichéd as it might sound, this makes it obvious that it's the journey and not the destination that counts. No matter how much you desire to be thin, rich, healthy, get promoted or get married, the thought of doing it by hating every day and wishing for it to be over faster is as painful as it gets.

But there's a big difference between 'hard' and 'loathing'. A workout is difficult by default – it's how it's designed. But ask me to stay fit by doing a type of exercise I hate, and I'll be unfit forever. I don't like dancing at all, I don't feel good doing it, and so you can sell me the best program that promises to make me slim and fit through dance, and the answer will be no – unless someone has amazing selling skills, which will probably result in me buying the DVD and never using it. (Yes, I've done that plenty of times.)

Similarly, people have a hard time following their meal plans because all they contain are salads with no dressing. We're not goats. No wonder you would want to skip your planned lunch and order takeaway instead when the food you prepped is not suitable for human consumption. I'm a vegan, I love salads, but those don't deserve to be called that. Every goal has its own version of fat-free salads and of course you want to quit if every meal is yet another serving of rocket. Thanks but no thanks.

Here are my favourite tips to make the journey more enjoyable:

→ Focus on what you're gaining instead of what you're missing out on. In some cases, this is only temporary. Plus, 'missing out' is only an interpretation, and so is discomfort. Life right now, good or bad, is only comfortable because it's what you know, even if it's not good for you; even if it's painful, it's a pain you're already familiar with – you've been living together for a while. Trying to change your present circumstances triggers fear in the survival part of your brain, which tries to stop you so you can be safe. Safe is good. Safe is comfortable. This will happen regardless of how positive the results might be, and it's good information to have, so you know what to expect.

→ Choose joy. Do the workouts you love, pick your favourite healthiest meals, improve your environment so that even if the task is unpleasant you can still enjoy being in the moment, reward yourself for the difficult phases, and find ways to love yourself through the process. Even when the activity itself is not enjoyable, you can still give yourself some well-deserved TLC. Treat yourself with compassion and understanding, and make sure your needs are met.

→ Break it down – set milestones, then monthly, weekly and daily goals, so you can get a regular hit of dopamine.

Dopamine

Dopamine is the chemical of rewards – your brain releases it both when you expect a reward and when you get the reward – and it produces pleasure. It's the neurotransmitter that helped humans evolve by helping the brain learn what feels or tastes good. It keeps us happy and, unfortunately, hooked to pleasure. Can't have only one piece of chocolate? Blame it on dopamine. Can't stop at one episode of your favourite show? Still dopamine. Every time you learn that something produces pleasure, your brain will push you to get more of it.

When it comes to your projects, dopamine can keep you motivated. You know you feel the excitement when you set a goal and then when you achieve it. But what happens in between? Scheduling daily tasks and short-term goals will allow you to tick those boxes and get a boost of pleasure on a regular basis, without having to wait until the overall goal is achieved. It will improve your confidence in yourself and your success, and give you a sense of accomplishment that not many other feelings can compare to.

Though there will be parts of the story you won't remember fondly, you don't have to win the prize for the suckiest journey. Find ways to make it pleasant and you'll acquire an essential skill for unlimited personal growth – the ability to embrace discomfort.

One step at a time

When you set a big goal that you can't even wrap your head around, the safest and most comfortable choice you can make is to be overwhelmed. It's a common and sensible response of your brain to protect you from danger. A new project is scary, difficult, uncomfortable, and of course you'd rather stay inside the comfort zone, doing what you already know how to do.

Overwhelm is never created by the project, the multitude of tasks or the size of them, but by how you choose to think about the situation. Nothing is fundamentally overwhelming or stressful, but your thinking makes it so.

The first thing to do is pause and take a breath. Seriously, when your mind starts spinning and obsessing over the difficulty of the task, the best action is to pause. It's in the pause that the magic happens. You breathe, calm your system, give your mind space to switch from spinning into problem-solving, and then take the first step.

I see all goals as projects, and so every big dream becomes a list of milestones and tasks that are small and achievable. 'Project management' sounds much more doable than 'working on your goal', and many of us in our jobs wanted to be project managers. Now you have that chance. However, you don't have to plan everything down to the tiniest details.

Though it's helpful to have an overall view of the whole path, it's not absolutely necessary. When you add your destination into the satnav, you get one quick glimpse of the whole journey, but then it switches to the one-step-at-a-time view because that's what you always need: the next step. Occasionally, accidents or traffic jams will prompt it to reroute you, and then it quickly goes back to showing you just the best next step.

Goals are no different. Thinking backwards from the end result, ask yourself where you'd have to be halfway through the journey, a quarter of the way, at the end of the month, at the end of the week, and then trace it back to today. What should you do today to find that successful moment a year from now? Take that action, no matter how small it is, and having set the ball rolling, you've switched from merely thinking about the future to making it happen.

Planning is a mix of having an overall picture but also enough space for creation, intuition and sometimes chance too. As time goes by, you will develop new relationships, start collaborations, partner-ships, and say yes to opportunities that you can't plan on showing up ahead of time.

I use the one-step-at-a-time approach in all my goals, from marathon running, which is literally one step at a time, to weight loss (one pound at a time), to saving for a new home (one thousand at a time), to reading 50 books in a year (one at a time), drinking two litres of water a day (one glass at a time) and so on. Some steps are faster, some are slower, and some need to be broken down even more. When writing a page is difficult, I split it into chunks of a hundred words. One single paragraph was all I needed to start writing a book.

TAKE ACTION

When your goal is overwhelming, use this simple four-step process:

1. Become aware you feel overwhelmed and remember that it's your brain's normal response to possible discomfort and change.
2. Stop and take six deep breaths, in through the nose and out through the mouth.
3. Knowing that overwhelm is a choice you're making with your mind, make a different choice.
4. Find the first easy and achievable step you can take, no matter how tiny.

And just like that, you're in it. Keep going.

THOUGHTS TO PRACTISE

→ I can do hard things.
→ Discomfort is taking me one step closer to my goal.
→ Even if it's uncomfortable, it doesn't mean it's wrong for me.
→ One step at a time.

Chapter 11
Fear of external opinions: what will others think of me?

It's terrifying to think that listening to opinions thrown out there without much considera-tion can influence your trajectory. And after everything has been shared, they go home to live their life, and unfortunately, you might do the same, instead of living your own.

While there's value in receiving and taking on board feedback from those qualified to give it and that have been asked for it, there will be plenty of clueless Uncle Joes and random Karens from the Internet commenting 'this is terrible' on your piece of art or online video. It's how the world works, and you cannot stop it.

Not everyone will understand what you're doing, who you're doing it for and why, and spending your time explaining it in every conver-sation will be a waste of energy. Whenever you start receiving unsolicited advice or opinions, use the following three questions to filter the words and decide what to do with the information:

→ What do they know about this?
→ Who are they talking about?
→ What do I believe?'

'What do they know about this?'

Imagine yourself being lost in a new city without a map and needing directions. (Your phone's battery just died – you're not a cave person.) You head straight for the first friendly-looking human you see and ask how to get to the place you're expected to be at. In the best-case scenario, they take out their phone, look up the address on the map and they give you an exact route. You memorise as much as you can and off you go.

Then there's the one who doesn't give you specific street names and how many lefts and how many rights, but knows the place and at least points you in the correct direction. You start to move knowing that you're getting closer and you can ask someone else later. Finally, worst-case scenario, there's someone who says 'I have no idea, but I would go this way'. What do you do? You would probably quickly dismiss the blind guess and ask someone else.

But what if it's a family member or your best friend and it's about your big life goals which they should be on board with because they love you so much? When it's someone you love and trust, who you go to for advice or support most of the time, it's hard to accept that maybe, in this case, you only need to trust yourself and a new group of people who will understand. With new goals, it's inevitable that you'll also join new communities.

My mother still doesn't know what I do. She doesn't understand business and thinks having a job is best. She doesn't get how I make money each month. She will probably never read my book. And that's OK.

As any other naive new entrepreneur, I was excited in the beginning to tell her all about it. I tried to explain my ideas and how I planned to make them happen, but all I got back was 'if that's what you want...'

And, in that way, I'm extremely lucky. She might not have been as excited as I was, but she was supportive in her own way, and not everyone is the same. I'd rather have silence and a change of conversation rather than 'Are you sure? I know someone who tried this and failed' or 'I don't think it's a great idea – give up before it's too late'.

Whenever Mum asks 'How's work?', more to be polite than from genuine interest, my usual reply is 'It's going well,' (even when it isn't) 'how's the weather there?' And I respond just the same when it comes to weight loss, marathon running and other goals of mine that she doesn't understand.

I learned that with certain people, certain conversations are not meant to happen because the results are rarely positive, and I keep those for specialised groups: I only talk about business in business groups or with a coach, I only talk about running with runners, and so on.

Having a goal can feel lonely sometimes and you'll want to talk about it. Choose wisely though. Better to feel lonely for a while than quit.

'Who are they talking about?'

I love horror movies. They don't usually scare me, and even when they do, it's a mix of excitement, laughter and jumping out of the chair. But that's my opinion and it's based on past experiences, how I was raised, how many horror films I've watched and generally what I like and dislike in life.

My friend Michelle hates horror movies and she thinks they're disturbing; she avoids them. One that I called 'fun', she called 'scary'. Was the movie fun or scary? Neither. The movie was fun for me and scary for her. Without someone to interpret it through their lens, the movie is neutral. If ten people watch the same film, you'll hear ten different opinions. But what's true? For each of the ten people, their own opinion will feel true to them, and that's the case for everything in life.

When you tell someone that you want to lose weight and they say it's hard, it means it's hard for them. Business is risky... for them. Writing a book is a waste of time... for them. We all see every event or idea through our own life goggles, which filter circumstances through all we know – people, information, past events, preferences and intuition, which are of course different from one person to another.

When I was getting ready to move from my home country to England and the bags were already half packed, I went out for lunch with a few friends. I was moving for a job, but my then-boy-friend-now-husband had to quit his to come with me. With only one scheduled interview, all he had was trust in his skills and the certainty of our relationship. During that lunch, someone at the table said this: 'I don't think it's a good idea to leave your job and go to London for work. I know someone who had to come back home because they didn't find anything. It's hard to get a job in London.'

With the information he had and his own life circumstances, our friend had decided that moving to England without a job was a terrible idea. We had no doubts and responded by simply stating that we'd figure it out. We had already done the maths with as much information as we could find on the web, and one income would have been enough for us to live on.

That wasn't the only conversation my husband had in which he heard how reckless, immature, or stupidly in love he was with me to decide to leave a fantastic career behind. We do wonder sometimes... what if? What if he had listened? We wouldn't have created this wonderful life we're living now. We talk about it sometimes and even if it's only in our imagination, the conse-quences of making decisions based on other people's beliefs feel terrifying. The conversation always ends with us being grateful for the courage to trust our own intuition and to live for ourselves.

It's terrifying to think that listening to opinions thrown out there without much consideration can influence your trajectory. That words that the speaker didn't even put much thought into can make you question your own decisions. And after everything has been shared, they go home to live their life, and unfortunately, you might do the same, instead of living your own.

Since then, both of us have learned to ignore by default. When we decided to live on a boat for a while, we announced it to our friends and families and then curiously watched them react to the news. It's fun to freak people out, especially when you're certain about your decision. You can always decide to be certain. Certain that you will always make the best decision for yourself, and no one else can do that because they don't live in your mind or your circumstances.

Parenting is an area where this becomes painfully obvious. Newly promoted to the roles of mum and dad, my husband and I have moments when, even if it's half-joke, half-pain, we say we're glad that our little one only has one grandparent.

In a new family, each one of the parents comes with their own beliefs and experience. And each one of the grandparents brings their own baggage. Right in the middle, there's a child that hears as many as six different opinions about any topic, or, with a bit of luck, only two, coming from the two extended families.

There is no manual for how to perfectly raise a child; everyone does their best, which looks completely different from someone else's. As I do with everything else, I decided that only one source of information is enough. If the child has any symptoms of disease, I look them up on the NHS website. I picked one parenting methodology and I apply the rules at home, and we enrolled P in a nursery that follows the same principles. I put blinders on for opinions coming from anyone else. If there's no right or wrong, I simply decide what right means for me.

'What do I believe?'

If someone told me two years ago that I'm a terrible writer, I would have probably stopped writing. I had my own doubts and even if I was constantly trying to improve, most times I wasn't proud of the pieces I created.

I believed I was a terrible writer and someone else saying those words would have only confirmed what I already thought about myself.

However, the same words wouldn't affect me today. I don't believe I'm a great writer (yet), but I also don't believe I'm terrible. Through intentional skill development and experience, I have already written some successful pieces, from articles people loved to email campaigns that created a lot of money. And this book, of course.

You don't react to someone's negative opinion unless there is something in it that you already believe to be true. When people confirm our own doubts, it's like finally finding the evidence we've been looking for. 'I knew it; I shouldn't be doing this.'

You will always have doubts. That you're not ready yet, the time's not right or you're not capable of making it work. But no matter what you're still unsure about, this is something I'm certain of: it's almost impossible to set a goal you can't achieve. Your brain would never let you even think about an idea that is completely out of reach. When there is desire, it means that something inside of you is already prepared for it.

Any skill can be developed. Any strategy can be learned. You can 'get ready'. (Though you'll never completely feel so.) There is nothing that can prevent you from succeeding except for your own mind telling you lies. Feeling like an imposter is always an indication that you care and you're on the right track. It means you're aiming for something better.

It's like applying for a new job. No one gets a job they are 100 per cent ready for. Typically, employers would send back a rejection response stating if the candidate was overqualified. But the candidate would rarely apply for such a position because there would be no challenge, nothing new to learn. When we do our jobs effectively and efficiently, it's usually time to aim higher and look for something else.

When scanning through a job description, you want to tick a few boxes, but not all of them. You know that the rest can be learned while doing.

When you doubt whether you're the one to achieve this goal, ask yourself why that would be true. Get practical and list all the skills that will help you be successful. And then, list the ones that you don't yet have and how to learn them. Finally, list the steps you need to take, or at least the very first one. Once the plan is more tangible, some of your fears will disappear. Keep the pieces of paper and go back to them every time you doubt yourself again, remembering that there was one day when you were certain it was possible.

You'll never feel ready

I'm often asked how I knew I was ready to quit my job when I did. I have to be honest here and tell you that I usually lie. I say that having a solid budget and a plan gave me the confidence to do it. And while that is true, I had a good level of certainty, I never felt ready. I still don't feel ready.

Feeling ready is an illusion. It's a moving target, and so you never reach it. There will always be a new book to read, a new certification to get, a new course to go through, a new experience that will give you more confidence. It's tempting to keep going because it feels safe. While in learning mode, nothing can hurt your feelings and it gives you a false sense of growth.

After looking at the lives of successful people, I learned that if you wait until you feel ready, it's already too late. My decision to quit was based on a mix of confidence in my own abilities to figure it out, a plan, a budget and some experience. There is no *ready*, but there's *ready enough*.

I felt ready enough. I didn't think it was reckless. At that point, I had gone through business training, I had got my yoga teacher certification, I was teaching one class a week and covering other teachers whenever I could, and already dabbled in online business with a blog. Looking back now, I can confirm that I had no idea what I was doing. The experienced, current me looks back at the newbie and thinks: 'Girl, you didn't even know how to write an email!' At the same time, I know that I wouldn't write emails with the quality that I do now if I hadn't started then.

However, if I look even further back, I'm glad I didn't quit my job when I first had the thought. There's ready enough, but there's also not ready enough. It's the difference between someone with a plan and someone who jumps from a plane without a parachute.

'Ready' is a moving target, and you'll never reach it. But you can reach ready enough. Learn what you need to get started, prepare a plan that's sufficient to know the first few steps, and then have trust that you are the person to get it done. Because so far, you have a fantastic track record.

TAKE ACTION

Brainstorm the skills and qualities you need for your current goal. Make a plan to develop them.

THOUGHTS TO PRACTISE

→ New goals, new communities.
→ I can love and respect someone and not listen to their opinion at the same time.
→ I trust I make the best decisions for myself.

Chapter 12
Making decisions

There is no right decision. There's only the decision that you make right.

A quick search on the Internet will reveal the shocking claim that we make approximately 35,000 decisions every day. What's even more jaw dropping is that an average of 221 of them are about food (Wansink and Sobal 2007). Both of these numbers seem extremely high, but that's because we're not always conscious of the micro-choices we make throughout the day. Yes, some are obvious: 'What should I have for lunch?', 'What should I wear?', 'It's already 6 pm; should I still go for a run?' But others are not perceived as decisions because they happen quickly, like whether to answer a call from an unknown number (the answer is no most times, am I right?).

You can see how this can easily tire your brain, and so making fewer decisions can help you reduce the overstimulation of your mind and conserve some of the energy that gets wasted through the thoughts and emotions that come with the decision process. It's not only the number of them that can get you exhausted though, but also the fact that some of them will be postponed and thought about for a lot longer than needed.

Choosing quickly is a skill that can be developed in time, and it will make life easier and a lot less stressful. But it's understandable why you might procrastinate over committing to one thing or another: the present situation is safe and you have no idea what's on the other side. You might also think that there's a right or wrong decision, and you can't risk choosing the wrong one. Staying where you are will protect you from any possible negative consequences that you will have to deal with.

'Right' and 'wrong' are, just like many other labels, interpretations rather than truths. The result of your action is always neutral until you have an opinion about it. You can choose to believe that whatever that result is, it's either what you wanted or what you needed. Both the success and the lesson are favourable to you, never against you. It sounds like a version of 'everything happens for a reason', but instead think of it as 'whatever happens, I'll be OK'.

The thought adjustment that made the biggest difference for me was this: 'There is no right decision. There's only the decision that you make right.' You choose what you feel pulled towards the most and do your best to make it successful. Even when it doesn't work according to plan, moving forward is still forward. You've gone past the indecision, and you will have more experience; you can also try a different option having new information – there is a lot to learn from a bad decision. The more you do this, the more self-trust you'll build. The more self-trust, the better and quicker the decisions.

I also have one more piece of great news: no decision is final. So far, apart from bringing new life out into the world, there was no other action I couldn't revert if I wanted to. There is almost nothing in your life you can't do anything about. You chose a job you're not happy with? You can change it. Your dropped out of college and now you want to get your degree? Go back to school. Unhappy marriage? Get a divorce. Did you buy a house too big for your wallet? Sell it and downsize. Life is too short to stay stuck in regret. Experiment. Make mistakes. Change directions and keep making bad decisions until you land on a really, really good one.

Pros and cons lists

In the personal development world, you'll find two types of teachers: those who are all about strategy, and those who are all about mani-festation, energy and intuition. My opinion sits somewhere in the middle. I know the power of taking calculated risks and understand the difference between reckless decisions and intuition. There will be times when you'll lay it all down on paper and decide that it's not for you. And there will be times when the list says something but your gut says something else.

A few years ago, I had to make a decision about moving to the United States for work. It would have been a nice increase in income, a new, exciting life, and plenty of doors opening up for me. I made a pros and cons list. The decision on paper was clearly in favour of going, but the only two items in the cons column weighed a lot more than the others. I decided to stay. Though I occasionally ask myself what life would be like if I lived in Seattle right now, it's always with curiosity, not regret.

Simplify everything

The second most useful piece of advice that I can give you is one we hear a lot from successful people – reduce the number of decisions you have to make. It's why we see so many tech entre-preneurs wearing jeans and a black T-shirt every day – they save their brain power for the bigger issues that need their attention. You can implement this in your life in two ways: planning and self-im-posed rules.

Planning

Planning is essentially a decision that you already made and can stop thinking about. I learned the power of this tool back when I was losing weight and realised how much of my time and brain power was spent thinking about food. Even if I wasn't fully aware of it, every time I passed by a pastry shop, I made a micro-decision: 'Should I go in and get a sausage roll?' Sometimes it was a yes, sometimes it was a no. I was free to choose in the moment, and there were multiple moments like this every day. Once I started planning what I was going to eat, usually for the whole week ahead, all these micro-decisions disappeared. And every time I caught myself thinking about food that wasn't on my list, even if just out of habit, I reminded myself of this new way of doing things and moved on.

When I noticed the impact this had on my mental chatter, which was significantly reduced, I started applying the same strategy in other areas too:

→ Planning the week in advance massively reduces procrastination and confusion about what's next on my to-do list.
→ I follow an exercise plan so I never have to wonder what I should do each day.
→ Whenever I need extra help, I choose a hybrid solution – a step-by-step program or a service provided by someone else that can reduce my need for thinking. For example, instead of stressing about what to post on social media, I use daily prompts created by an expert. I still think about what to write, but a lot less, considering I have a starting point and a direction.

Rules

If you're like me and you love discipline, you'll also love this idea. If not, you have my permission to skip to the next section. You might still want to give it a chance though, since this will simplify your life and give your brain a lot of extra room to think about important problems. Because just like planning, rules are decisions you make ahead of time, or at least create enough constraint that you are required to make fewer decisions.

Back when I was training my first puppy, I learned an interesting fact about dogs: they thrive when you impose rules. Instead of constantly asking themselves 'Should I jump on the bed?' and pacing around looking for some confirmation that it's OK, they know right from the start that the bed is off limits (well, these are definitely not my dogs). That gives the dog peace and allows her to relax. When they know exactly what they're allowed to do and the rules are consistently reinforced, dogs are happy. Your brain might be a lot more evolved than a dog's, but if I go back to my story about the mental chatter around food, I can tell you for sure that once I added some restrictions, the chatter stopped and I had peace.

Even those who present themselves as free spirits and live every day from moment to moment will follow at least some rules imposed by society, religion or law. Marriage is a great example of limitations we happily choose to accept: we go out with, kiss and sleep with one person only – if not, we get in trouble. And it's not a decision you make every day; it's one that you make once for a lifetime (or until it stops working). Not only does getting married make us happy, but most people set it as a goal. I too wanted to find someone and settle down because dating was exhausting, and I had had enough of breaking up and making up.

Rules exist everywhere. They make the world work. And life is so much easier when you voluntarily add a few. They work in all areas, including diet, environment or work, and they can save you time, mental energy and, in some cases, money. Here are a few of my own to borrow or use as starting points:

- → There are no animal products in my diet, and no alcohol either. (This makes shopping a lot quicker.)
- → My wardrobe is very simple, with pieces that work combined in multiple ways; I only buy clothes in certain colours and styles.
- → I don't work on Saturdays.
- → I never comment on posts on social media about controversial subjects – e.g. veganism, politics, vaccines.
- → I exercise every single day. (Rules can be positive too!)

Some rules can be seasonal and useful for months or years at a time. As with any other decision, rules don't have to be final either. For five years straight, I didn't have any fizzy drinks. One day, as a result of a pregnancy craving, I stopped the streak and have had them, on and off, since that day. Once a rule stops helping you, you have the freedom to change it.

TAKE ACTION

What could you plan and what rules can you add to your life to decrease the number of decisions you need to make every day?

Bonus
A couple of questions that can help you make a decision when you're trying to choose between two possible options:

→ If both were successful, which one are you pulled towards more?
→ If money wasn't an issue, which one would you choose?

THOUGHTS TO PRACTISE

→ There is no right or wrong decision.
→ Whatever happens, I'll be OK.

Chapter 13
Journaling for overthinkers

*Whenever I don't have a personal
coach, I turn to pen and paper to create
a mirror for my thoughts.*

Deep thinking is one of your superpowers. There is, however, always a risk of getting stuck in a loop, processing the same thoughts over and over again, or burning out because your mind never takes a break. For that, I want to help you get started with my favourite, most accessible and affordable tool for overthinkers: journaling.

Types of journaling

Journaling has plenty of benefits for mental and emotional health, and it can be used in many different ways – there really isn't a right or wrong way to do this:

→ It can reduce stress, worry or other negative emotions by providing a mirror for the thoughts that are creating them.

→ It can be a way to unload your brain on a daily basis to create more calm.

→ It can be a tool for self-discovery, helping you explore your beliefs and the effects they produce in your life.

→ Or it can be a non-active participant in a conversation,

while you pour your thoughts down on paper to feel better after a bad day or during a difficult time.

Morning brain dump

The simplest way to get started with journaling is to give yourself ten minutes in the morning to write. It's completely pressure free, the only purpose of it being to get everything you're thinking out on paper. When you wake up in the morning and your body is just starting the engine, your mind can go into overdrive. You'll start thinking about what you need to do, remember events from the day before, plan dinner, reflect on a dream you had or start worrying about an important meeting. Write it down – you will feel better and because some of those notes free up your mind from having to remember tasks/events/plans, you will start your day feeling calmer and more prepared. On those mornings when you can't think of anything to write, simply start with 'I have nothing to write' and repeat it as many times as you need to, until your brain starts producing thoughts.

Reflection

While the brain dump is dedicated to creating mental space, reflection is for reducing negative feelings about a person, an event that happened recently or the actions you're taking towards a goal. You can do it in the evening of the day the event happened or the next morning, and you describe what happened by focusing on your feelings and thoughts. Knowing that it's your own interpretation that's causing you to feel a certain way, you can read back and separate facts from opinions. You'll also identify exactly what can be changed in order to feel better.

This was my main tool while I was losing weight. It was like having a coach. Even now, whenever I don't have a personal coach myself, I turn to pen and paper to help me navigate whatever I'm going through. Here's how a short line from a journal entry looked like back then: 'Yesterday I had chocolate and felt guilty about it. It's probably because I believe chocolate is bad.' Though very simple, you can see how I was able to find out why I was feeling guilty. It was also an opportunity to work on believing that no food is good or bad, and that a piece of chocolate doesn't hurt, just as eating one single salad won't help too much.

Another journal entry I remember very well because it had an impact on my future was this: 'I'm upset that she didn't give me any classes at the new studio. I must be a bad teacher.' Back when I was teaching yoga, the owner of the studio I was working for opened a new location, with some new teachers, but also with some of the existing ones. I wasn't offered a class there, which triggered a lot of thoughts about why that might be true. As the human brain is biased towards looking for danger, mine went straight to the most negative thought it could possibly think: 'I'm a bad teacher.' I was indeed a beginner, but I had plenty of students who loved my classes and I knew that. I challenged myself to look for positive reasons, knowing that unless I asked the owner for the true reason, everything I thought had an equal chance of being true. What could I think to feel better? These were some of my answers: 'From a business perspective, having more new teachers is great for the customers', 'There are newer teachers than me who deserve to be given a chance', 'My students love my classes', and 'I'll always be available to cover classes, but I get to have the light schedule I have now for longer'.

You can also use this type of journaling during more stressful seasons, for example during a fight or after a conflict. If you're anything like me, most fights happen in your mind only, without ever saying anything to the other person for days. Relationships involving two introverts must have the quietest fights. However, while neither of you is ready to talk yet, take some time to look inside your thoughts and pick some that will help you feel better.

Self-discovery

If you're working on a specific area of life, you can use writing to find some of the limiting beliefs you have around it, so you can understand your behaviour and create long-lasting change. Beliefs lead to actions. Actions led to everything you have now and can create everything you have been longing for. This type of journaling can also help you find patterns in thinking or the history of a certain belief.

'Money' is a great example, one that multiple books have been written about (*You Are a Badass at Making Money* by Jen Sincero (2018) and *Chillpreneur* by Denise Duffield-Thomas (2020) being a couple of my favourites). If you were to start understanding your behaviour around money and your ability to change how much you're earning, you could begin by answering a few questions on paper:

→ What do you believe about money?
→ What do you believe about rich people?
→ What do you believe about yourself and your earning capabilities?
→ What are some stories you remember about money from childhood all the way to this moment?
→ What did your parents teach you about money?

While the list is by no means exhaustive, it's a great starting point for your self-discovery journaling. You can use something similar for any other topic: business, work, being an artist, changing careers, education or your identity, to name a few. You could also go through this book and answer some of the 'Take action' questions at the end of the chapters.

Creative journaling (or prompts)

You might find it easier and a lot more creative to start with a prompt. My coaching clients love to get some of these as 'homework' after our sessions, to challenge their thinking or push them to see new solutions to their problems. If you'd like to try journaling as a new habit, here are ten of my favourite prompts (you can always search online for more):

1. Describe your best self. What does she do for work? What habits does she have? What does she believe? What are her qualities?

2. It's three months from now and your current goal is achieved, or you made great progress. What's life like? Ask your future self to tell you how you did it.
3. As your future self, write a letter to your present-day self, thanking you for all the hard work you've done while you were working on your goal.
4. Write a letter to your 15-year-old self.
5. Think about your last three big accomplishments and find your secret success formula. What were the qualities that made you successful? What were you motivated by? What steps did you take? What were the emotions you were feeling? What support did you get? What obstacles did you encounter and what solutions did you find?
6. Write a letter to someone you want to ask forgiveness from, even if they are not alive anymore.
7. Think about a successful person you admire and a problem you have right now. How would they solve it?
8. Write a 100-item bucket list.
9. Find at least ten reasons for each: I am brave because… I am strong because… I am confident because…
10. What would you like to create and experience in the next ten years?

If you're thinking about trying journaling, there are a few things you can do to build the habit:

➜ Start small – ten minutes per day is more than enough.
➜ Choose the time of day with the greatest potential for success – when are you most likely to be available for your new habit? If you already have a morning routine, stack this new habit on top of it.
➜ Get a new, cute notebook; I know you won't mind a trip to the stationary store!
➜ Don't judge your progress; there is no right or wrong way to do this.

TAKE ACTION

Try one of the journaling methods I suggested. Set a timer for ten minutes and get writing!

THOUGHTS TO PRACTISE

➜ Everything I have or don't have is down to a belief, which I can change.

PART 3
SOCIAL SKILLS

OK, my friend, it's time to face the dragon. So far you have: learned how to set up boundaries and say no to what you're not interested in or comfortable doing; learned how to understand thoughts and emotions; and developed the ability to cope with or reframe circumstances. Now you're ready for the challenge: developing people skills and confidently diving into situations that would otherwise make you cringe. This part of the book is filled with practical advice to help you feel comfortable asking for help (through hiring, delegating or just asking for favours), networking, selling, meeting new people, speaking in public and leading a team.

This is the last piece of our puzzle. I'd love to believe that with the skills acquired in the first two parts, you now have a lot more time, energy and courage to take action. By setting loving boundaries you not only protect your calendar but also your physical energy. When you stop overthinking and learn how to process feelings, you protect your mental and emotional energy. You have the proper setup for what I know will be hard, but necessary work.

You can't always achieve challenging goals on your own. Let's learn how to connect and communicate with others, build the best support team possible and succeed beyond the level you have experienced so far.

Chapter 14
Worthy to ask, open to receive

I know you're strong, but strength can only take you so far. Your willingness to ask for help in the key moments and your openness to receive it are what will help you thrive.

If it feels unsettling to have people doing you favours, helping you out or even providing services you paid them for, I get it. I used to be that girl who cleaned before the cleaner came. In this chapter, we'll look into why this might be difficult and what to do about it. Just as we needed two big thought adjustments to say no ('I'm good enough' and 'I can't change what others will think of me no matter what'), you need one more helpful thought to ask for help without feeling guilty or undeserving: 'I am worthy and open to receiving.'

Deserving of attention

During one of the first few private coaching sessions I ever had, my coach asked me why I told her not to send me anything via post when we signed our contract. When she onboards a new client, she likes to send a care package in the mail, a gift to say thank you. I asked her not to. The irony is that when someone pays me that amount of money, I'm willing to buy them a car! Yes, not a *card*, a *car*!

'Because I don't want to inconvenience you,' I answered. She looked at me like I'd said something ridiculous. And it was. You know how good you feel when you send someone a present. We all love to imagine their faces as they unwrap the surprise gift. She gave me a minute to think and it all came back to me. It was a pattern.

I remembered that when I was in the hospital having the baby, I asked the midwife not to bring me anything because I'm a vegan and I don't want to inconvenience anyone; though a potato with baked beans is hardly an inconvenience. I never buy anything for myself until my husband convinces me that it's OK to do so. Or begs me, should I say. I'm almost afraid to ask for help from someone whose job is to do just that because I always feel like I've done something wrong. I expect them to yell 'Who do you think you are to ask this of me?', even when I pay them.

'Because I don't deserve it,' I said.

And then I paused and cried for a few minutes. My next words were, 'That is so sad.' It is sad to think of yourself as fundamentally flawed. That you're not worthy of a simple gift or attention, let alone success and money. It's heavy baggage I've been carrying since I was a child. Except for my family, everyone I met – from teachers and doctors to store cashiers – made me feel like they were wasting their time with me. This was the culture I grew up in, and it broke me. Everything, including love, had to be earned. If it didn't hurt, it wasn't good enough. But in the same way as feeling good enough should come as a birthright, so should feeling worthy. Otherwise, it's also a moving target. You'll never get there.

There are multiple ways in which this can show up in your life:

- ➔ feeling like you're doing something wrong, or that you're in the wrong place and someone will eventually call you out
- ➔ overworking so you can feel you deserve your pay check
- ➔ having a hard time asking for a favour
- ➔ you'd rather do everything on your own, just so you don't have to 'inconvenience' someone else

→ you clean before the cleaner comes over

→ even when you do pay someone, you want to help and make their job easier

→ you feel like an imposter in any leading or managing position

→ you always look for evidence that you're a fraud, and when you make a mistake you think to yourself, 'I knew it'

→ you buy gifts for everyone in the family, except for yourself

→ you feel guilty any time you get a gift, spend time on your self-care or buy yourself something expensive.

I wish I could tell you that I have a clear solution and you can fix this right away. I don't. Something that you've been conditioned to think for a long time won't change immediately. However, being aware of it is the first step. Knowing that it's part of your default thinking and recognising where in your life this is likely to show up will help you prepare for situations in which it has the potential to limit you. When you expect it to happen, it gradually stops becoming a problem. The awareness that it's a default response, but not necessarily the truth, will help you take action even if it won't feel good. Actually, your body will feel resistance (e.g. sweat, tight chest, a lump in your throat), but that doesn't make it wrong. Don't worry; it gets better in time.

How to change a belief

Humans are born with very little. Apart from needing the connection with their mother, shelter and food, babies live in a state of bliss. They are enough as they are. They deserve all the attention and the sleepless nights. They have no self-doubt and no fear. All they do is receive, and they receive openly. This means that all the beliefs you have as an adult came with practice, by reinforcing them over and over again until they became part of you. Through experiences and what other people have told you, you have a set of brain pathways that now light up automatically. A belief is a habit of thinking, and all habits are the same thing – connections in the brain that get stronger with repetition.

Think about an action you do automatically, like locking the door when you go out. You know it's a habit because you don't need to think about it anymore – though you did do it while learning to lock the door as a child. You've probably experienced the 'Did I close the door?' panic multiple times because it's hard to remember doing it. But yes, it was closed every time. Think of this automation like the linking of two brain cells every time you were on the outside of the door and locking it. The first brain cell is your location (outside, right next to the door), and the second is the action (locking the door).

Every time you locked the door, connecting these two elements, you created a bridge between the two cells. With repetition, the bridge became stronger and stronger, and harder to destroy. Now, when you're outside the door and that first brain cell is activated, the locking-the-door brain cell is automatically activated too because experience tells your brain that these two come together. You may have done it purposefully the first 100 times, but now there is no need to consciously think about it anymore.

The question is, can that bridge be destroyed? The connection between your neurons can become weaker and eventually fade with time if unused. If this wasn't true, no one would be able to change any behaviour or any thought. But change requires awareness of what the behaviour is, and what it's caused by (its trigger). In the example above, the trigger was the location (outside the door), and the action was locking the door.

If you wanted to change the action, say leave the door unlocked, you would have to bring awareness back to the situation: plan your exit, purposefully stop yourself before locking the door, and choose to not lock the door. In this case, in this simplified explanation you've just introduced brain cell number 3: not locking the door. Every time you manage to remember and choose the new behaviour you want, you create a new bridge, between cell 1 and cell 3. At the same time, the one between cell 1 and cell 2 becomes weaker. From here on, the more you repeat the new action, the more the old one loses strength.

Stop, choose, repeat.

CELL 1 = "outside"
CELL 2 = "lock door"
CELL 3 = "don't lock door"

What you need to have in mind is that this process is anything but smooth and quick. You'll often forget completely, some other times you'll lock and then immediately unlock the door, and occasionally you'll get it from the first try. The important thing to remember is that it gets better in time and change is possible.

Going back to beliefs, your route to change is paved with repetition. Firstly, you need to become aware of your triggers – in what situations in your life might you be stopped by thinking 'I'm not worthy'? When the trigger happens, what do you want to think instead? Then, give it time. The trick with beliefs is that you're not even aware of them in the beginning – I bet you don't walk around thinking 'I don't deserve anything!'

Just as you're not consciously thinking about locking the door, walking, turning on the lights when the room is dark, driving your car or choosing a favourite seat on the train or bus, beliefs run on autopilot too. It would be great if the automated ones were 'I'm the queen of everything', 'I'm the smartest and most beautiful', 'I deserve all the fame, money, success and love in the world' or 'I can do and be anything'. But they're not. They're the sucky ones like 'I'm not good enough', 'Good girls are seen and not heard', 'Rich people are evil', 'Don't rock the boat', and hundreds of others that we've been hearing repeatedly during our early years until they were stored in our minds as truths to wreak havoc during adulthood. Though that was the case for me, 'I'm not worthy' might not be your reason why asking for help is difficult. It might just be that you were raised to always give but never get, or to believe that you'll look weak if you can't do it yourself.

When you first discover the effects of these beliefs in your life, you feel the urgency to fix them, and at the same time a frustration towards those who've been feeding them to you. You can drop the frustration. In some cases, you won't know exactly who and when caused you to think this way, and dedicating time to remember is counterproductive. As I was trying to figure this out for myself, I discovered that it's not one single event or one single person, but multiple ones. I've been told repeatedly that 'I'm not entitled to anything', that 'I need to work hard to earn money, respect or love'; I was asked 'Who are you to ask me to do anything?' or yelled at on the phone (or in person) by service providers I interacted with, including store cashiers, school nurses, teachers, postal office employees… and the list can go on and on.

Trying to find the culprit, or make a list of people you need to forgive, is a waste of time and energy. I made my peace with it by noticing that in a way this has served me well, and probably you too. Though it is now creating a plateau in your progress, it's also made you a hard-working, polite, generous and considerate person. They're all good qualities to have, even if the vehicle has now stopped being useful.

And so, all you need to do is to decide that from now on, that faulty thought pattern needs to change, and you're committed to doing the reps (a term from exercise training, i.e. the repetitions). Stop and say your ABC: Awareness, Breath and a new Choice of thought. When you're in a situation where this can become a problem, remind yourself of it, interrupt it and respond with a 'Thank you, but I know it's not true', 'I'm a good person', or a thought specific to the situation. This is nothing but a conversation between you and your brain. After it's been telling you lies for decades, you're finally talking back.

Next time someone sends you a gift, stop and watch how you're feeling. See it for what it is, a habit of your brain, and let it pass. Take a deep breath and choose to believe it's not true. You're a good person, I know you are. You deserve the gift.

Make life easier

You might wonder why this even matters because you can do it all on your own. I know you're strong and capable, but strength can only take you so far. You can summon it to push through the inevitable discomfort of the day-to-day, but your willingness to ask for help in the key moments and your openness to receive it are what will help you thrive. They will make life easier too – lighter and more peaceful. You'll let go of the responsibility to march on like a soldier when, really, a bit of support would completely change your experience.

I know it because I've come so far with this that I can recognise the big and the small wins alike. Even being sick used to be unnec-essarily hard. If I happened to feel like an inconvenience as a fully functioning human, imagine what needing care felt like. During my last bout of flu however, I caught one of these small wins and knew that something had changed for the better, forever. I didn't only accept help, but I asked for it and enjoyed it. As I woke up shivering one night, I realised that I needed water and some paracetamol, both requiring me to get out of bed and walk downstairs. But I felt so cold that I knew it was going to be very uncomfortable. 'Do I get up and power through? Do I stay in bed and let it get worse? Or... do I ask my husband to go get them for me?' I gave him a nudge and told him what I needed.

Of course I could have used strength and willpower to take care of myself, but there was no point in suffering. There never is. There is no shame in accepting help, and no prize for doing it all on your own.

THOUGHTS TO PRACTISE

> → I deserve to be here.
> → I deserve to *ask* for what I want.
> → I deserve the seat at the table.
> → I'm open to receiving help.
> → There is no shame in getting help.
> → Getting help doesn't make me weaker.

Chapter 15
Delegation: letting go of 'doing it all'

Time is your most precious resource,
the only one you can't get back once
spent. Delegation buys more of it.

You probably have a lot of resistance towards delegation, for multiple reasons. But if you want more time to do tasks that matter, more time to recharge and simply more time to live, you have to hand over some of your responsibilities to someone else. When I say delegating, I mean giving some of your tasks to others who can do them as well or even better than you – from hiring a cleaner or a nanny to take over some of the responsibilities at home, to hiring help in your business, or handing over tasks to your team at work.

When I'm asked how I do it all, my answer is simple: I don't. I have a nanny, a cleaner, a virtual assistant, an accountant, a designer, and I hire contractors whenever I need help with a task I either don't have time for or I'm not very good at. It wasn't easy. Letting go of control, especially for those activities that you either do very well or find enjoyable, requires some willpower. The first step is to acknowledge that if you want time for the needle-moving tasks, those that create the most value and progress, you must let go of some of the others. Your time is your most precious resource, the only one you can't get back once spent. Let's get more of it.

The main reasons for not delegating

'No one does it as well as I do'

When I clean the house myself, I believe it looks better than when someone else does it, even if they're professionals. Of course I believe I do it better because I get to do it exactly how I want to. However, I'd rather spend those hours working on my business or going out for a walk to relax. It's a compromise that I'm willing to make, so I can use my time in a better way. I've been living in my current house for almost two years, and I can honestly say I have no idea what the back of the cupboards looks like. I managed to let go of control, so I can focus on what really needs my attention.

'I can't afford to pay someone else'

In some cases, this is true, but what really matters is what you do with the time you get back. Here's some simple maths, with randomly chosen numbers and activities. Let's say that for the work that you do, you make £50 per hour (assuming you're paid by the hour for your job, service, side hustle or business). However, you spend five hours every week cleaning the house. Those five hours are blocked, as you can't work while you clean.

You think hiring a cleaner is too expensive. However, let's say a cleaner is £10 per hour. Paying five hours to outsource this activity would cost you £50. Still, you decide to do it yourself. If you worked during those five hours, you would make £250. If you do the maths, by not hiring a cleaner, you potentially lose £200, but you have the feeling that you have saved £50.

Making your very first hire might require some effort because you can get stuck in a vicious cycle: you don't have enough to pay someone, which means you can't get more time, and so you can't make more money to pay someone. This is truly painful, but you have to break the cycle somehow, by either borrowing time from another activity or taking a leap of faith and investing in getting help. Do remember that this is an investment; you will get a lot more back in the long run.

THE MATH OF DELEGATING

Assumptions:

1h x Your Rate = 50
1h x Cleaner Rate = 10

If YOU clean for 5h	If you hire a cleaner
You spend: 0	You spend: 5 x 10 = 50
You make: 0	You make: 5 x 50 = 250
You lose: 250	You gain: 200!

'I want it perfect'

What may be the most difficult to get over is perfectionism. But sometimes, in order to make things happen, you have to let go of the idea that you're the only one who can achieve high quality. Or even more, that high quality means perfection.

I'm all for high quality, and I'm rooting for those aiming to do A+ work. As I'm writing this, there's a new movement against perfectionism, and I half agree, half disagree. Currently, one of the most common pieces of advice going around the Internet is 'Do B- work'. I understand the reason. Some of us are so afraid to get started that we use perfection as an excuse not to show up. Or we do get started but get stuck on the same step forever. In that way, a crappy first version is what you need to get going.

But unfortunately, most people stop at that crappy first version. They never go back to make it better. And so the online space is now saturated with bad videos, PDFs full of typos, and generally low-quality content. Even books are now more questionable, as anyone can publish one. It's OK to get started at B- because it gives you a playground, an opportunity to grow. Now that you have the crappy first draft, you can go back and improve.

But asking for help is not a guarantee that the quality will decrease. At times, if you're letting go of those tasks that you're not the best at, the complete opposite will happen. Be willing to let go of control for the sake of the final product. What do you want most? To release it into the world? To make it perfect? To do it all on your own? Whatever you decide will have consequences for your schedule, your energy and the overall timeline of the project.

How to delegate

What helps the most when delegating a task is making a clear request, with clear instructions and expectations. It's the best way to ensure there will be no back-and-forth and you'll minimise the need for interaction. Whenever I decide to give someone else the responsibility of a task that I've been handling, I write down every step with as much detail as possible. If it's a digital task, I record my screen while performing all the actions in the exact way I want them done and talking through every click. With admin or routine tasks, this is the easiest way to get the result you want.

Don't make any assumptions about the other person's understanding of the task, and overexplain if necessary. Ask them if they need any more details and confirm your agreement. If that's an option, offer to shadow their first attempt, or ask them to shadow you before handing over the work.

In a job, documenting what you do will come in very handy when it's time to delegate. Write down steps and create how-tos or templates, so that it's easy to organize a handover. Make it so easy to understand and copy that you're always ready to take a long holiday without creating chaos in the company or home. You can do this preparation in the background, without having to talk to anyone beforehand. Then, when needed, if everything is ready, there's little you have to communicate verbally. Though you need to initiate the conversation, the written or recorded instructions will back you up and answer all the possible questions for you.

When you start delegating in this way, your impact will increase. Everything you used to work on is still happening, but you're also taking on new work. If you've ever said 'I wish there was more of me', 'I need another me' or 'I wish I could duplicate myself', this is the way to do it.

What to delegate

In any role, there will be the activities we call needle movers and those we call distractions. The needle movers are those that take you one step further, and they can only be done by you.

In a leading role, creating a vision or making decisions are needle movers, but admin work like creating spreadsheets or organising your calendar are distractions. If you're an engineer, writing code is your needle mover. But if you're transitioning to a managing role, that same activity will become a distraction. When you're home-schooling your child, activities related to their education are needle movers. Cooking dinner at the expense of spending time on the curriculum is a distraction. However, when you're a cook, that distraction changes to being a needle mover.

Distractions are not necessarily unpleasant; you might love to immerse yourself in creating budgeting spreadsheets or working on the website of your business. I do. But they are not the activities that produce results for you. The Pareto principle says that 80 per cent of the results are created by 20 per cent of the activities. When you're short on time and energy, your focus needs to be on the 20 per cent. The rest can be delegated or… they'll just have to wait. If something doesn't impact the quality of the result, and no one would notice if it wasn't done, then you can free up even more time by removing it from the to-do list completely.

What can be delegated:

- → needs to get done but you're terrible at it and you hate doing it
- → needs to get done, you're good at it but you hate doing it
- → needs to get done, you're terrible at it but you love it
- → needs to get done, you're good at it, you love it, but it takes away time from the needle movers.

If you don't get to work on the needle movers – those tasks that take the project or your career forward – you'll make little to no progress. The needle movers are yours to take on, and no one else can execute them better than you. Make space for them, and let other people work on their own needle movers. What's a distraction for you is the bread and butter for someone else. I know you're a top performer in many areas. But others are too. Give them a chance.

TAKE ACTION

What's one task you can delegate right away?
What's one task you know you'll have to delegate in the future? Start documenting it.

THOUGHTS TO PRACTISE

- → Delegation buys time. Time creates money.
- → For something to be made better, it has to exist first.
- → I let others work on their needle movers, so I can work on my own.

Chapter 16
Favour debt

Energy in, energy out

There's another type of asking for help, and in this case it's free. It's called a favour, and introverts are running away from it like it's a ghost because, in a way, it is. You believe it's going to come back and haunt you until you repay it. We all suffer, at different points on the scale, from favour debt fear. It's the terrifying thought that once someone helps you, you'll have to do the same for them, and ideally with a gesture of the same value. Otherwise you'll live with shameful debt and an unclear conscience.

This is yet another faulty thought pattern we learned from childhood, even though, at its core, it had positive intentions. Humans should be thoughtful and help each other out; it's how we evolved, and after all, it's the nice thing to do. But keeping score of it is not.

As I was growing up, my mother used to go to most of the weddings she was invited to, even when she didn't want to or it was challenging from a schedule or financial point of view. It wasn't just because she absolutely loves a party, which she does, but to get 'favour credit'. In our culture, if you attend someone's wedding, they must come to yours or your children's. She was making sure that when the time came, those people or their offspring would come and celebrate with me, whether I knew them or not.

Energy in, energy out

If you believe this is an extreme example, I agree with you, though we behave in a very similar way in other parts of life too. However, we pay a lot more attention to some than to others. When you drive and give way to a pedestrian or to another car without being in a position where you're legally required to, I bet you don't follow them around so they can eventually do the same for you. You believe that it's the right thing to do because you're a kind, considerate human being.

Those exact pedestrians or drivers might not be able to ever pay you back, but others will. Someone else will give way to you when you cross the street or enter a roundabout even if it's not technically your turn yet. The balance is always restored, but not with the same people. See, when I think about favours and humans helping each other out, I think of it as points of energy in and points of energy out. The accounting department of these points is internal to each one of us, and it's independent of who helps you and who you help.

This is the only way this system can ever work, so that humans retain their ability to be kind without expectation, but also because it's impossible for you to know who you've impacted indirectly. Your actions have ripple effects that you might not know of. Helping someone can enable them to help someone else. You will never know how a simple gesture can influence not only one but multiple people, which is why you should only be concerned about the energy that goes in and the energy that goes out and give and receive openly.

If you find yourself at the supermarket and the person that's in front of you in line is five quid short, you might want to jump in and help them. You don't expect them to get your number or bank account details and pay you back; you wave them goodbye and happily add to your 'favour credit' so that, in turn, someone will jump in when you're in need. If they insist on paying you back, I bet you'll say: 'It's OK, just pay it forward!'

If you're indeed dealing with someone who keeps count, the whole relationship is questionable. There should never be a requirement for you to repay the favour (unless that's the deal) or respond to a gesture of the same value, which is not specific either. You can't put a number on the impact your actions have. If someone drove you to the airport one day, which is worth, let's say, 100 points, is it OK to take them out for drinks twice, each worth 50 points? Or is making small talk 10 times enough, each being worth 10 points? Nonsense. Energy in, energy out. It's the only way we, as a society, can function without keeping scores or calling each other out when we're in debt.

If you're having a hard time applying this concept to your whole life, compartmentalise it – keep the balance for the different areas like work, family, friends, and then the rest of the world – charities or volunteer work, organisations, hobbies. Also, there are seasons when you receive more than you give, and that's OK too.

Expressing gratitude

You might be wondering how you can live with the thought that someone has done you a favour you might never repay. Well, you can say thank you, send a card or some flowers or show in some way that you appreciate it. Silent gratitude and sending them positive vibes whenever you think of them are just as good. It is, after all, all about energy.

When I was in high school, during year 3, I took part in a history contest as part of a team. The contest was a very big deal for our history teacher, so we worked hard and did well – we won third prize. To receive our certificates and congratulations, we were invited to the president's residence, the Cotroceni Palace, which is the Romanian version of the White House. That meant a trip to the capital, which was for us an extraordinary event.

One of my teammates was also my best friend, so I rode in her car, driven by her dad. We stopped to have breakfast midway and while chatting in the bathroom, reapplying the grown-up make-up we were allowed to wear for once, she casually mentioned, 'Wow, this morning I almost forgot my ID – you know we're not allowed to pass security without one!'

To which I replied: 'Oh, no…'

I did it. I forgot my ID. What so far had been an exciting, but at the same time relaxing morning now turned into panic. This was 2005, so technology wasn't yet so advanced as to fix our problem at the touch of a button (or multiple buttons, if you were hip and had a BlackBerry). I told my history teacher, and then called my mum. My mum then called my teacher's daughter, who owned a fax machine (remember those?) and ran to her place to send it over. My teacher also knew someone at the palace who could receive the fax, so we fixed the problem in a couple of hours. I got in.

The rest of the day went perfectly, as we all soaked in the attention and admiration we got. I felt guilty for all the trouble I'd caused, of course, but I believed I deserved the help. In the end, I brought my teacher fame and appreciation. I didn't think anything of it anymore until my best friend told me a few weeks later that our teacher was very upset with me for not going to thank her daughter, who went out of her way to help me. 'At least she could have sent a card!' she said.

Now, at age 33, yes, I would send a card. But expecting a 16-year-old to show appreciation in any other way than a 'thank you' is unreasonable. At the ten-year high school reunion, I met with the history teacher again, and guess what?

She came to me and asked: 'Do you remember that time when we went to Cotroceni and you forgot your ID? We had to ask my daughter to fax it to us.'

'Yes, miss, I remember.'

I thought a few times about asking around for her address to send some flowers. But I think I might just wait until the 20-year reunion when she'll probably remind me again.

I was grateful, but I didn't know how to show it in a way she'd recognise as good enough. And this will always be a risk, but how you feel about it will still be in your control. Expressing gratitude in an extroverted way might be expected by other people, but so are many other activities we don't do. With your new-found sense of worth and confidence, send a note, text, email or some flowers and let them know, in your way, that you appreciate the help.

There will be times when a kind gesture is offered just because. Times when they'll help because they have to. Times when they'll be happy to help and times when they won't. People who keep score and people who don't. Times when you'll think nothing of it, and others when you'll overthink it for no reason at all. Times when you'll go above and beyond to repay the favour, and they'll still not consider it good enough. If someone is keeping score, that's their choice to make and you cannot control it. You can choose not to care; you can choose how you feel; your thoughts are up to you.

Once you see yourself as worthy of receiving and let go of the idea of 'favour debt', your life will change in more ways than being able to ask for help. You'll openly receive compliments; when you're told that your hair looks nice today, the default reaction won't be 'Oh, no, it doesn't' but 'Thank you so much!' You'll let those who genuinely want to help do it without drama; just open your arms and receive it. You'll stop overthinking every time you need to ask for a favour because you know you maintain the balance anyway; you're a kind human being who helps others and deserves to be helped occasionally. You will stop keeping score too because there is no way you'll ever fall short. You're earning points every step of the way by helping others, and through the ripple effect your kind actions have for them, their families and even the world.

THOUGHTS TO PRACTISE

→ It's out of my control if someone keeps score.

→ It's OK to show gratitude in a way I'm comfortable with.

→ It's OK if this is a season of life when I need to receive more than I give.

Chapter 17
How to ask so the answer is yes

Whether you sell a product, ask for a favour from a friend or try to convince your child to eat their greens, the rule is always the same: show what's in it for them.

Have you ever bought a workout DVD from a TV ad? They're so good, I should probably ask how many, not 'if'... I almost bought a Zumba pack even though I hate dancing! And don't even get me started on those magical mops that clean tile grout without any product... But can you imagine the effect the ad would have without the before and after stories? Would you ever go to the gym if they didn't sell you the possibility of a hot, healthy body that enjoys life and effortlessly runs up the stairs? Would you say yes to an offer that sounds like this?

'Join our VIP membership for £120 a month. We know it's a lot of money, but this is how much we need to charge to make a profit. For this price, you'll be able to lift heavy weights, sweat like a pig and be sore for days. You'll also miss your favourite TV shows and your restful evenings will now be spent with us at least two or three times per week.'

I'm being sarcastic, but this is what an honest advert would look like. We go to the gym for the results we'll get, not for the exercises. We might love the company, the location, we love the feeling we get after a good workout, but if you think about it, moving your arms and legs while carrying heavy objects is by no means an interesting activity. If there were no benefits, most people would stop doing it.

Everything you do willingly, you do because you'll gain from it. Everything you buy is because of how it will make you feel or look, or who you'll become in the process – happier, fitter, more successful, calm, relaxed, a better parent, the best version of you, wealthy, more knowledgeable, satisfied.

Similarly, it's the special food that grandma cooks that makes you go to big family gatherings, even though you're not a fan of Uncle Tom and his 'when I was your age' stories, and you dread being questioned about your relationship (or lack thereof).

When you're looking for a new job, you stop at the job listing that advertises the best benefits: salary, time off, the new skills you'll acquire and opportunities for advancement. During the interview however, it's what you give back to the company that sets you apart from the other candidates and earns you the job. They care about their benefits. Whether you sell a product, ask for a favour from a friend or try to convince your child to eat their greens, the rule is always the same: show what's in it for them.

'We'll be able to move whenever we want to if we don't like the neighbours, we'll take long walks with the beagles in new areas, be closer to nature, and if you want, I'll call you Captain!' is how I convinced my husband to sell everything we owned and buy a narrowboat. And it sounds so good, we'd do it again today.

Humans are selfish: they care about themselves the most, so when they don't identify or resonate with a request, they're less likely to say yes. But if you show the benefits, it will seem like you're the one providing the favour, not the one asking for it. This will make it a lot more comfortable for you to ask, and a lot easier for them to accept.

How to use this at work

I'd been asked by one of my clients for advice on how to present a new project to a team member in order for them to feel motivated.

First, here's how not to do it: 'Corporate thinks it's important to work on this project. If we're successful, it's going to make the company a lot of money, so it's on the list of priorities for this year, and possibly next year too. They asked us to cover all the admin work, and the first phase is due to be completed in November. Should we get started on Monday?' Now that you know more about how to ask, you probably found some issues with the request above. And you unfortunately also recognise it as a very common way to approach task assignments.

Here's what a skilful manager would say, and what I suggested my client try: 'I have a new, very exciting project you'll want to get involved in! It will give you a lot of visibility and you'll acquire new skills that will help you get the spring promotion you're working on. It's very aligned with your yearly goals and I feel it will allow you to shine and use some of your superpowers. Corporate is very interested in the success of this project, which means we'll get rewarded nicely if we deliver well. I have no doubt that you can do it. I also know that you love a challenge, and you have the opportunity to automate a lot of the work because you'd cover the admin tasks. And don't worry, you won't need to be in too many meetings. Prepare some nice reports and send a weekly update because I know this is the way you express yourself best. Do you want to catch up on Monday and get started?'

The employee would be a lot more excited in scenario number 2. Though you can still assume from scenario 1 that it's an important project and the rewards might be worth it, it's not explicit. The company seems to gain the most, and the rest are merely details that the team member doesn't even need to know immediately. Plus, doesn't admin work sound boring?

In scenario number 2, all the focus is on the employee and what they're getting – a task that will help them with the promotion they're working on, the opportunity to show their talents and a challenge to keep the job interesting. Even if admin work is usually boring, their manager found a way to make it less so. But apart from the benefits, the employee is also getting some compliments and the confirmation that they're valued and understood. When the company is mentioned, it's still in a way that will show the team how big of a deal the project is and how lucky they are to be a part of it. I can confirm that this was a success and the employee replied to the email from the manager (my client) with 'I'm in!'

Maslow's hierarchy of needs

No matter who you ask, consider what they might be getting out of it, and focus on that when you make the request. The gains may be obvious but some of them aren't. If you're wondering what the rewards may be, one way to analyse the situation is through the psychologist Abraham Maslow's hierarchy of needs. This is used in psychology to understand the motivation behind human behaviour, and it's described as a pyramid.

At the bottom, you can find basic needs such as water, food, comfort, rest, safety and security. The level above represents love and connection to others. One step higher we find self-esteem or significance, and right at the top of the pyramid sits self-actualisation.

The lowest level has great impact on someone's life. If the basic needs are not met, no one can even focus on the ones above. They cannot move forward unless they have a solid foundation to live on. You may occasionally help meet these needs by paying someone for a job that provides and covers the bills or gives them a sense of comfort and safety. But more often than not, the ones higher up the pyramid will be of interest.

Once the low-level needs are fulfilled, humans become more motivated by the top levels: belonging to groups as part of the need for connection; challenges, achievements or attention to feel significant; and anything that will help them grow to get them closer to self-fulfilment. This is why it's difficult to keep someone doing the same job forever – it might pay the bills, but if work relationships are not positive, they're not recognised or they don't grow, they'll be looking to find these somewhere else.

Going back to the new project proposal, the manager's request ticks a few boxes:

→ it makes the employee feel important and understood
→ it will help them get new skills and get promoted
→ there will also be some external rewards expected (money)
→ it sets a challenge that the employee will be excited about
→ it removes worries and provides a setting in which the employee feels safe
→ connection with others is present, but in a way that's comfortable for the employee.

Though we are talking about admin work, which is by default considered boring, it's packaged in a way that will meet the employee's needs, so they're more likely to not only say yes, but to thank the manager for the opportunity.

To know how to phrase your offer, you have to know what the other person wants or needs, and this is where one of your superpowers is very helpful: listening to and observing other people. I know you're not a fan of chitchats or long conversations, but you can always turn them around to become monologues – theirs. Whenever you can in the conversation, ask questions and let them talk. Again and again.

It's what makes hairdressers or taxi drivers make chitchat. Showing an interest in you is something that every service provider has to learn how to do. That's what makes you feel good, listened to, and will in turn result in a generous tip. For extroverted clients, I'm sure this works very well. For us, not so much. But now that you know the secret, you can flip the questions, have them talk more, and you can rest and enjoy your haircut.

TAKE ACTION

→ Where can you apply these principles right away?

Chapter 18
Influence and leadership

When you change someone's thinking, you change how they feel and how they act. When they change their actions, they change their life, and that is something they will never forget about you.

You might not ever have considered yourself a person of influence, or perhaps you feel that introversion means that you can't be a leader. After all, leaders have to speak in public, ask their teams to work for them and always be visible.

Actually, being an introvert has nothing to do with your skills as a leader, and it definitely doesn't mean that you can't be a person of influence.

Introverts make great leaders. Your ability to listen to yourself and others, observe people and your deep thinking are superpowers when it comes to leadership. You are able to create powerful visions, plan and strategise, and you're a great judge of character, which means you'll make good hiring decisions – at least most of the time. The rest is a skill. And like any other skill, it can be learned and practised until it's part of you.

Influence is not about manipulation; it is not about convincing someone to do something they don't want to do. Influence is about helping people take action that will benefit them, and most of the time you too. You use influence to increase your impact, and help people make the decision to trust, listen to, follow or buy from you. Here's a great exercise to understand my definition of the term.

Look back at your childhood and remember that one person that you now say had an influence on you or gave you some of the best memories. A parent, grandparent, nanny, teacher or a neighbour that took care of you. And answer this: Why did you pick them? How did they make you feel?

The answer, for everyone, will be something along these lines:

→ they made me feel important
→ they listened to me
→ they believed in me
→ they encouraged me
→ they motivated me
→ they paid attention to me and were present
→ they taught me something important.

For me, it was my neighbour from the second floor that took care of me for a few hours after school, before Mum got back from work. I was, from 12 to 4 pm, the most important person in the world for her. She made my favourite meals for lunch, and always had a Milky Way for dessert, even though they were very expensive. I got so much attention that, in turn, I was incredibly well behaved with her. She was also the one to have the difficult conversations with me because I listened. This, in a nutshell, is influence.

When people feel supported, understood, listened to, if they can see how a certain action will benefit them, if they trust you and believe in your mission, they will say yes. Here are three ways in which you can increase your level of influence – you can use these principles in a corporate environment to motivate your team, in a business to sell or build community or at home with the kids.

Show people you understand them

No matter where you stand on politics, whether you like, tolerate or dislike some politicians, it's an area that offers us plenty of examples when it comes to influence.

In 2004, Barack Obama spoke at the Democratic convention, when no one knew who he was. But that 16-minute speech made him known. After introducing himself and briefly telling the story of his diverse family, he spoke to everyone that was ever to hear that speech in a way they understood and made them feel seen: to every parent that can't afford medicine for the kids, every senior who has to choose between paying for rent or medical care, to families of soldiers and the soldiers themselves that do more for the country than the country does for them, and to young people who have potential but not the money to get into college.

He gave them hope. He painted the picture of an America that really is the land of opportunity, and a government that's meant to offer support and serve. He wanted everyone to see him as one of their own, or, as he put it, 'a skinny kid with a funny name that believes that America has a place for him too'. Even though back then he wasn't even speaking for his own candidacy, everyone agrees that that was the speech that made him president.

Show you care, in whatever way works for you. Use words people will understand and that make it obvious that you understand their problems. It's simple but powerful enough to make you president.

Change the way people think

I know I went on and on for an entire chapter about how you cannot change how someone thinks. Though it is still true, and in some cases it's not worth your time, if you're a leader (whether that's of a community, a company or a household), you will occasionally have to change people's beliefs or show them a different perspective. It's what I'm trying to do myself in this book – show you how to think differently, so that you can remove your old limitations and get to the next level.

You can also change how someone thinks by teaching them a new skill, technique or topic. When you change someone's thinking, you change how they feel and how they act. When they change their actions, they change their lives, and that is something they will never forget about you. Most of my mentors have been influential to me in this way. I learned to think differently about myself, my abilities, what's possible for me, and I shifted all my beliefs about money, self-worth, confidence, jobs, entrepreneurship and many others.

A few years ago, after spending most of my adult life trying diets and seeing my weight go up and down an annoying number of times, I discovered this thing called 'coaching'. Through a recommendation, I started listening to 'The Life Coach School' podcast, and its host, Brooke Castillo, talking about eating and our relationships with food in a way I had never heard before. I gave it a shot – what did I have to lose anyway? Not only did I finally reach this goal that had eluded me for so long, but I also found a new way to help people and a career I love. And so, through initiating a change of thinking and teaching me the skill of coaching, Brooke has become one of the most influential people in my life.

Motivate people to take action

You can do this in multiple ways, and you might also notice that the previous two techniques apply here too. One way is to lead by example. It doesn't have to be explicit; you just have to be the best you can be and let others observe you. There's always someone watching; there is always someone you might influence, even if you don't know it. The most obvious example is children. Our kids don't do what we say; they copy what we do. But so are others.

Back when I had my fitness blog, I was sharing updates, reviews of classes I was attending, pictures from runs or before-and-afters. Though back then I wasn't very good at blogging, or at writing in general, I got plenty of comments either congratulating me or thanking me for the motivation. The best kind of messages were the unexpected ones though. Every now and then, someone who I hadn't heard from in years messaged me to say what an impact I had on them with the blog, and the changes they'd gone through because I shared my story. They never commented on the blog and never liked a picture on social media, but they did the work in the background and got results. This is the power of leading by example. I know you'll resonate with this because we introverts are lurkers on the Internet. We rarely comment or like a post, but we read it. We see it all from behind the curtains. And just as you watch others, others are watching you.

However, in many cases, you don't have to take any action for your community to do so. Sometimes, all you have to do is tell them, directly or indirectly, that you believe in them. That they can do it. Belief was shown to have an impact, on students in particular, through a few studies done throughout the years. In the 1960s, R. Rosenthal and L. Jacobson (1968) conducted an experiment in which they told teachers that certain children had scored higher on an IQ test, and they were expected to perform better than others. Though the IQ test was made up, and in the beginning, all students had the same chances of success, the ones the teachers believed in more did perform better.

And lastly, there's creating a vision that people believe in. A vision for the world, or themselves, that can keep them inspired and motivated. In Ashlee Vance's biography of Elon Musk (2016), we get to see what this means in a company. Though Musk is pictured as a genius with unreasonable expectations from others, and employees from both his companies are overworked, they are still happy to be part of his world. They believe in his vision and work relentlessly to create it, whether that's reducing climate change at Tesla, or expanding the human habitat at SpaceX.

Vision is what's used in selling too. Even buying this book was prompted by you creating a vision of the future in which you are successful, good with people and still an introvert at heart. Next time when you see or listen to an ad, get curious about what's actually presented in it. Is it the product? Rarely. It's a better future.

THOUGHTS TO PRACTISE

→ Introverts make great leaders.
→ Influence means, first and foremost, caring for and understanding people.

Chapter 19
Can introverts sell?

Selling is nothing more than communicating that you have the solution to someone's problem. How it's done makes the difference between a great shopping experience and feeling pressured to buy.

Introverts most certainly can sell. And now that I've given away the answer from the first line, let me explain why introverts make great salespeople.

Neither extreme introverts nor extreme extroverts do a great job at closing the deal. On one side of the spectrum, there's too much talking. On the other side, too little. Extroverts can blow the sale by being too friendly and too talkative, not leaving enough space for the other person to express their needs and offer insights into how the conversation should go. Introverts can appear apathetic, shy, and hence easy to say no to.

According to studies (e.g. Grant 2013), the sweet spot on a scale of 1 to 7 (1 being extremely introverted and 7 being extremely extroverted) is 4.0. Quiet people should make an effort to intervene more and extra popular Joes should shut up and listen.

There are three qualities of the introverted personality that will be of great use while you're trying to sell something: observing, listening and empathy. While most of your pitch will be prepared and rehearsed ahead, the human standing in front of you is unique and no conversation can be scripted in so much detail as to take into account every possibility. So once your potential client is standing in front of you, your observation skills will help you notice their reactions and change your pitch accordingly.

Allowing some silence is great too, and you're the best at it. When you let the person think about what you're saying and comment out loud, they will tell you what they like and what they don't, what they need and what they don't. They might not say so specifically, but you're a great listener and can read between the lines.

Empathy is the ability to understand how the other person is feeling and respond to it in a considerate way. When you can relate and adapt to the feelings and gestures of your potential client, they will sense you have a deep understanding of their needs. And when people feel listened to and understood, they buy.

Selling mindset

After a few years of running different businesses, I too can confirm that yes, we can sell. And there are ways nowadays that make it a lot easier, with my favourite example being email marketing. I love telling stories via email, which is creative, pleasant, introvert friendly, and so far, has worked for me no matter the industry. You can absolutely find a way that works for you and develop this skill through repetition... once you move past the default reaction of hate towards selling.

I get it; I grew up being told bad things about salespeople too. I had the impression that selling is sleazy and pushy all the way until I had to sell my own services. But selling isn't sleazy and pushy; people are. We blame the tool for how the tool is used by some humans.

If you think about it, everyone is selling all the time, albeit not specifically. Your partner sells you on how good your relationship is, the kids sell you on ten more minutes at the playground and you sell yourself on your daily habits. The money transaction may be missing, but persuasion techniques are still being used by all of us, all the time.

Still, many of us have generalised our opinion about sales, even though our spending habits tell a completely different story. I may have had this subconscious belief that selling is sleazy, but I didn't mind buying 12 pairs of colourful yoga leggings on one single shopping trip. I will happily go into a store selling items I love and even hope to have a shop assistant help me pick something out. Not all the selling we experience is negative. Actually, most of it isn't. Do you feel pushed when you buy your groceries? Do you feel cornered when you see an ad online and you decide to click and purchase? Even a book cover is a sales pitch, a thoughtfully crafted page, specifically designed to make you buy; and we're all so grateful it's doing a really good job.

Selling is nothing more than communicating that you have the solution to someone's problem. How it's done makes the difference between a great shopping experience and feeling pressured to buy. That only depends on the salesperson, and you don't have to use any technique you don't agree with. But if you love the product and you're convinced it will help solve a problem, you're doing your fellow humans a disservice by not telling them about it. Selling is caring.

Selling tips from successful introverts

During my research for this book, I interviewed a successful introverted salesman with 15 years of experience. He shared a few tips on how to balance being great at this job and nurturing our personality:

→ Only sell products you love. When you believe that what you're selling is of great value and will help your customer, it feels necessary to make the offer. Otherwise, it will feel like lying and we're not very good at that.

→ Write down your pitch and rehearse it in advance. There is nothing wrong with that. Give yourself time to prepare.

→ If you're going on business trips, make sure you get some time alone too. Skip a breakfast or a dinner out and give yourself time to recharge.

→ When you get a no, look at it objectively – why did it happen? How can you do better next time?

→ Don't take it personally. No one is saying no to you, but rather to the product.

→ It gets better in time even if you can't see that happening yet. Keep practising.

Your sales persona

I have one more tip for you, one that helped me when I was starting out and I had to be more comfortable in situations where I was put on the spot. And while my example will be specific to a sales role, know that you can apply the technique to any social interaction. The inspiration came from hearing about Beyoncé and her alter ego, Sasha Fierce. At the beginning of her career, Beyoncé was very shy and felt awkward dancing freely and wearing the clothes she was supposed to wear on stage. So she invented this persona named Sasha Fierce who took over when she was ready to perform. When she eventually became comfortable with her new status, Beyoncé merged these two personalities and publicly announced that Sasha was gone.

When 'performing' is uncomfortable, pretending to be someone else can help you detach from the situation and get the job done, at least while you're getting used to it. I first used this technique as a receptionist at the yoga studio where I was also teaching. My shift was on Saturday morning, during some of the busiest classes on the timetable. However, part of my role also involved pitching to new customers coming to try a class, or making follow-up phone calls to those who didn't make a decision on the spot. This was so far outside my comfort zone that I couldn't even see my comfort zone anymore.

But I remembered this role-playing game and figured that if it was good enough for Queen B, it had to work for me too. 'What if I just pretended to be someone else today? What if I acted like the best salesperson I know?' I tried it. As I was opening the door on Saturday morning, it felt like going through a metamorphosis, replacing my usually shy, less visible self with this new persona who could chitchat and sign people up for memberships. Let me get this straight: I had business training and I knew exactly what I needed to do and say, but my energy wasn't matching the job. I used this exercise to borrow, just for a few hours, the personality of someone I knew who was successful at this job and I was able to observe. On some days, it felt like an acting job rather than a receptionist one, which was also a helpful way to look at it. Because once I closed the door behind me and went home, I also left that way of being behind, like an actor changing out of their costume after leaving the stage.

THOUGHTS TO PRACTISE

→ Selling is caring.
→ Introverts make great salespeople.

Chapter 20
Networking

You can't lose at this game: you'll either make a friend, a valuable new connection, or you'll decide to move on without building the relationship, but it's almost impossible to create a negative result.

I have a confession to make. I came back to write this chapter as the last task before the final editing began. I felt, and still feel, inadequate to offer advice on something that on many introverts' lists of 'things to avoid doing' sits right at the top. Networking can be a great tool to make new friends inside a community, find a life partner, attend work conferences and represent your team or company, or build new relationships for your growing business. But if just thinking about it makes you feel tired, I have a few tips that will make it less overwhelming. I used to be a non-networker too, but in the last few months, I've found myself joining new communities, attending events (online), connecting with people on social media, and not only accepting to 'hop on a call' to get to know each other better but initiating the invite.

Ever since I started my business, I knew networking was necessary because it's the best way to expand your circle to find clients, friends of clients or friends of friends of clients. My elevator pitch was ready. I even knew how to find events, the theory of how to interact with someone new, and I had plenty of topics of conversation. I'm multi-passionate and skilled in many areas, so whether you want to talk about nutrition, fitness, books, software, electric cars, music or investments, we can probably find a subject that will keep us chatting for a while.

It wasn't happening though. I was making up any excuse not to attend a networking event because I couldn't see myself as the person who would spend their time surrounded by people instead of cosily reading a book at home. What I could imagine instead was hiding in the bathroom, pretending I'm interested in the food or drinks just so I have something to do, or awkwardly sitting in a corner looking around hoping that either someone will come and talk to me or that at least no one will notice 'the weird one in the back'.

But 2020 came with a blessing – most events moved online, and it offered us an opportunity to dip our toes and try networking in a more comfortable environment. I loved it and it gave me enough confidence to move things offline. The fact that it was through a screen didn't fix all my problems though. I've been in breakout rooms where I didn't say a word, I cancelled a few meetings, and stumbled through my words a lot in the beginning.

What made it work eventually was the new story I was telling myself. I was no longer making my introversion mean that I'm awkward and can't network. Instead, I approached this challenge with a new perspective: I told myself that networking is a skill, and right now it's difficult because I haven't done it before. When you see meeting people as a skill that can be developed rather than a talent you're born with, it becomes possible. No matter how old you are and what your story has been so far, you can decide to be a beginner and get better at it, step by step.

As a coach, I heard many times that you shouldn't make your past mean anything about your future. 'Nice quote,' I always thought. You can be told something again and again and never get it, until you do. It finally made sense. Just because I used to be bad at networking shouldn't mean that I will continue to be bad at networking. I started looking at networking just as I do at writing, business or fitness and I took the same steps I take with each new skill. If you want to try some of them, here they are.

1. Adopt a healthy beginner mindset

You can be a beginner at a skill in two ways: beating yourself up about it or seeing it as a game that you need to level up at. Because it's something new and potentially dangerous for your survival by your brain's calculations, it will do everything in its power to stop you, including showing you how much you suck. It doesn't feel good, it really doesn't. Being the one at the back of the room who has no idea what's going on while everyone else seems to be having a great time can make you want to turn around and go back into your comfort zone.

First of all, you're probably in the wrong room. Secondly, you can still choose to say kind words to yourself, be patient and look at every new try as objectively as you can. The only way to level up is to do it again and again, but better. And you can only do it better if you review what you did, find an area for improvement, and plan to implement the new idea next time. Every master was a beginner once.

And don't worry about embarrassing yourself – while you're still finding your feet, no one will even notice you.

After you have gone to your first one or two networking events or met a couple of new people, stop for a moment to give yourself a pat on the back. That was hard! However, event number 3 will feel a lot easier. Number 10 will feel easy. And when you reach number 100, it won't even matter that you're an introvert anymore.

2. Start your game at level 0

Any game starts at level 0 – isn't that great? As you're warming up to the rules, you have time to try all the tools while it's still easy. Your first step should always be one that you can take and can be successful at. How can you make it easy? Start by looking for communities or events that you already know or are low pressure. Maybe ask a friend to bring you along to one.

The first two events I ever went to, which were in person and happened before I did all the mindset work I'm telling you about, were pleasant experiences. One was a tech meet-up that I was invited to by a friend; it felt good to have at least someone I knew around. The second one was a meet-up for beginners to practise public speaking. Say what?! Public speaking. Knowing that it was for beginners reduced some of the anxiety because potentially everyone was bad.

As the world moved online, it got even easier to do this. If you're uncomfortable, you can leave the room with the click of a button and blame it on the Internet connection. You can mute yourself and hide the camera and write in the chat box that your microphone is not working. You now have a unique opportunity to practise this skill while it still feels easy. In the beginning, commit only to listening but staying in the room. On the next one maybe decide to introduce yourself. Join in on a conversation on the third. And so on.

Doing some practice rounds will prepare you for when you join an event that matters to you. You can practise the words you'll say, try on a few 'vibes' and of course learn how others do it. If you have a pitch you want to do, write it down and rehearse it before the event too.

3. Focus on one thing at a time

Every skill, networking included, has many aspects to it and trying to do it all at once can feel overwhelming in the beginning. There's paying attention to what the other person is saying and showing genuine interest; asking questions to start a conversation; introducing yourself and what you do; speaking or doing a presentation or hanging around during breaks. Attempting to be good at all of them at the same time is a recipe for disappointment. Start with one and get better at it first. Once comfortable, move to the next, and so on. Instead of being terrible at everything, start by being OK at one aspect of this skill.

4. Expand your view

You might initially be tempted to only look at networking for work, but your hobbies and passion projects can offer a brilliant playground before you take this people-meeting business more seriously. Having something in common with a group from the beginning will ensure there's always an interesting topic to talk about for both sides.

After moving to the UK, the first new friends I made apart from those I worked with were from the running club I joined. OK, 'club' might be an overstatement. It was a small group of people going out for lunchtime runs, organised by a store that sold running shoes. Yes, I bought four pairs of shoes during that first year and made my husband buy another three, but at least I got some extra time to chat.

Meeting someone new

Whether live or online, you might have to or want to meet someone and have a conversation with them. Since this change of mind that I had around networking, I started to organise plenty of virtual or face-to-face coffee chats with people I connected with during events or inside the communities I'm part of. Initially, it felt like I was someone else because it didn't seem real. Am I doing this? Who are you and what did you do with Andreea? I'm still very much the same person as before, only without a thought that wasn't helping me move forward in life: 'I'm awkward when I meet someone new.'

Once I stopped believing that thought, I asked myself why it was there in the first place. What don't I like about meeting someone new? What am I afraid of? What is it that makes me uncomfortable? The answer always started with 'I'm afraid they'll think I am…'

What if they think I'm stupid? What if they think I'm not good enough?

First of all, while you focus on your own insecurities, know that the other person probably feels the same as you do; it's hard for everyone! However, it's not what they think that matters to you. What you're afraid of is that they might be right. But through the new beliefs we built together, now you know that that's not true. You are a valuable human being with a lot to offer. This was the main shift that needed to happen inside me to accept invitations and even to reach out to other people: I have a lot to offer, and they would be lucky to meet me. I can help, I can listen and I can be a great friend. I'm doing them a service by showing up.

Once you see it as mutually beneficial, you'll feel good about asking someone to spend some of their time with you. Stop focusing on yourself and be there for them. Ask them questions and be genuinely interested in their answers. You can't lose at this game: you'll either make a friend, a valuable new connection, or you'll decide to move on without building the relationship, but it's almost impossible to create a negative result.

The energy-draining activity of talking can be an issue and this is where the power of asking questions comes in. Ask and listen; let them do most of the talking – unless they're also an introvert, in which case the conversation will be a lot more balanced. Also, don't forget about your people-time quota. Even with this new-found confidence in networking, the need for in-between time is not to be ignored. Too little of it will leave you emotionally exhausted and ruin your experience during the meet-ups.

Chitchat is not and will never be something I enjoy but if that's what is needed to start a conversation, I tell myself that I can do it because it's important. Remember the purpose of it is to eventually build close relationships and it has to begin somehow.

TAKE ACTION

Sign up for a networking event or join a community that can support you with a goal. What's your first step when it comes to networking?

THOUGHTS TO PRACTISE

→ I have a lot to offer, and they would be lucky to meet me.
→ I can help, I can listen and I can be a great friend.
→ I'm doing them a service by showing up.

Chapter 21
Public speaking

Anxiety is your friend. It's there to remind you that you're human and you have a brain that's trying to keep you safe. Nothing's wrong. There's nothing to fix and no reason to stop.

Imagine yourself on stage with 1,000 people looking at you, waiting for you to entertain or educate them. Did your stomach turn? Maybe. But here's what I want you to reframe: you're not nervous because you're an introvert. You're nervous because you're human. Anxiety before an event can happen to anyone and for many people it never goes away. What you want is to manage and befriend your anxiety instead of trying to get rid of it because that might never happen.

But what is this feeling and how can you handle it in the moment? Anxiety is fear of uncertainty; you're afraid because you don't know how it's going to go, and there's only so much you can control. You're also wondering what your audience will think of you, which should be less of an issue by now. Though you can prepare, rehearse and double-check the equipment, you have to live with the thought that you can't plan everything. However, instead of worrying, allow yourself to accept that you're human. You can also decide that no matter what goes wrong, you, together with someone else who can support you, will figure it out.

I never avoided public speaking and I love doing presentations, but I'm still nervous. Almost every time, a few minutes before it starts, all

I can think of is 'Why have I agreed to this?' Answering that question is extremely important for your performance. Why are you there? What do you want to achieve from speaking in front of an audience? Knowing the intention behind the activity will help you not only structure the talk, but give you some motivation when you want to back out, which will inevitably happen. It will also remind you that no matter what 99 per cent of your audience thinks, there is at least one person in the room who needs you to deliver that talk.

This thought process is part of my pre-presentation routine: I take a walk to clear my head and calm my nervous system; I think about who needs me and why it's important to go ahead; I breathe deeply and remind myself that I'm human and that it's normal to feel nervous. I sit with that feeling and let it flow, instead of pretending that it's not there and risking it will turn into a full-blown panic attack before the presentation.

There's a common piece of advice that recommends reframing nerves with excitement. This has never worked for me. I intellectually know that it's not excitement; it's fear. I'm excited too, but I respect anxiety enough to give it its own place. It's my friend, with me on each occasion, reminding me that I have a brain that wants to keep me safe and that what I'm about to do is completely insane. It is insane. So what?

But of course, apart from processing your emotions, there are a few practical tips you can apply to make it a success:

→ Start preparing the content ahead of time. Some of your ideas need a few days to be developed and improved to become the best they can be. Once you become an expert on a topic and talk about it again and again, this won't be as necessary. But in the beginning, it's useful to leave your brain enough time to refine the key points of your presentation.

→ Practise without and with an audience. You'll memorise some of the words, but it will also prepare you to make eye contact, use your body language and handle your nerves.

→ Develop the skill by practising public speaking without having a scheduled presentation. Attend beginner groups, get acting or improv classes, or any other activity that will be fun for you and can prepare you for delivering a talk in the future.

Raising your hand in a group

One of the most common pieces of feedback I received during my corporate career was to speak more during meetings. During the last review, as my manager was talking, I remember thinking, 'But I have nothing to say. Also, you guys talk too much and even if I have something to say, it's impossible to stop you.' When I had something to add to the conversation, I would do it, but otherwise talking for the sake of talking felt useless and exhausting. Not only did I not want to say more than needed, but I also believed others should talk a lot less. Do you know how they say there are no stupid questions or stupid opinions? Oh yes there are.

How much your voice is heard shouldn't be a measure of how much you're contributing. However, interrupting someone else or raising your hand in a group you're not yet comfortable with might feel challenging. I remember being in school and feeling these jitters when I knew the answer to a question and hoped that the teacher would call my name without me raising my hand. Sometimes no one else had the answer and I felt terrible for missing out on a great opportunity to get a good grade or at least some kudos. Later in life, this has translated into not sharing my knowledge with someone who needed it.

Thankfully, the online world has helped with this too. The tiny icon to raise your hand in a video meeting is easy to click and makes that first step more accessible. I still feel a bit of uneasiness and my voice occasionally shakes when I'm put on the spot, but repetition is the mother of all confidence. The more you do it, the less nervous you get, and we live in the best time in history to get your reps in.

There are three main reasons why raising your hand can feel hard:

→ You're not in the mood to talk. That's OK, it happens to us a lot and this will probably never change. The only thing

I'm asking you to think about is whether what you would say would change the perspective of someone else, the course of the discussion or even the path of the project. If your intervention would save a lot of time, consider this one extra push for everyone's sake.

→ You don't feel worthy of being there. Though I have already covered the topic in detail, I want to add this: if I know you at all, and I think I do, you are probably a fantastic person. You have a lot to offer, and whatever room you're in, they should be happy to have you. But beware of this sneaky, possible unconscious thought because it becomes reality if you give it power. When you believe you shouldn't be there, you don't add to the conversation. If you don't add to the conversation… you shouldn't be there.

→ You're not confident in your knowledge. If you resonated with my school story, then you too have a track record of holding information that no one else does. You're the geek who reads the footnotes, pays attention in class and does their homework. The one who immediately browses the web when hearing about a topic they know nothing about. Come on, we're introverts; we study for pleasure! Trust your instincts and jump in before they move on to talking about something else. The best way to work on this lack of confidence is to become excellent at what you do. Learn as much as you can and consider yourself an expert.

THOUGHTS TO PRACTISE

→ I'm not nervous because I'm an introvert; I'm nervous because I'm human.

→ I can feel anxious and do it anyway.

→ There is at least one person out there who needs to hear what I have to say.

→ I'm an expert and people will benefit from me raising my hand.

→ I'm knowledgeable – I study for fun!

Ending notes: your next steps

Thank you for joining me on this adventure inside the introverted mind. I hope I provoked your thinking and maybe even shifted some old beliefs that were keeping you stuck. If you want to take this work further, here are some ideas:

➜ Go back through the chapters and re-read the thoughts to practise. You can use them as affirmations, write them down in your journal or use them as prompts. Do you believe them already? If not, what do you believe instead? Spend a few minutes writing to notice what your brain offers on that topic.

➜ Go through the journaling prompts offered at the end of Part 2.

➜ Pick one social skill you'd like to improve and use all the ideas in the book to work on it.

➜ Work with me. Go to andreeasandu.com or email me at hello@andreeasandu.com and set up a consultation call. I'd be so happy to meet you and hear in what way The Introvert Who Could helped you change, and of course, take your personal development even further.

And before I say goodbye...

You are worthy.

You are good enough.

And you most definitely can.

Acknowledgements

If I really were to say thank you to everyone who deserves a mention here, I would have to write another book. If you've been part of my story in any way, I have probably learned something from you, and for that, I appreciate you. There are, however, a few names I cannot skip because they make up the support system that made *The Introvert Who Could* come to life.

My husband Alin, who made my coffee every morning and who throughout this book-writing adventure gave me the most precious gift – time. He's always my biggest supporter, and he sometimes believes in me so hard, I have no other choice than to go and do it.

My mum and my brother who are always on call. All I have to say is 'Help' and they're there for me unconditionally. Though they probably imagined a different life for me (many people did), they had to accept at some point that I'm just a little bit weird and I need to do things my way. Not everyone can do that. But my people are special people.

My writing accountability group – Jackie, Jinny, Liz, Carol, Paula, Karen, Diane, Tim and Karl – also known as the #ATeam. Michael Heppell, the one who created the Write That Book programme and the fantastic community that came with it, including the #ATeam. It was the environment that made me believe that maybe, just maybe, I could do this.

My friend Becky Karush, who helped me develop my writing in the past year through her weekly salons. She can see the good in everything, even in those pieces that I think have nothing to give. And for that, I'm grateful.

All my fellow introverts who took time to talk to me during the research phase and who of course I'll keep anonymous. You know who you are.

My support team at The Right Book Company, who made sure this book will be the best it can be.

And Kirsty, our nanny, who spent a little extra time with our overactive toddler, and helped me make each book deadline when it seemed impossible.

Because I have to end this list at some point, I'll finish by giving thanks to my coaching mentors, the people who trained me to be who I am today – Brooke Castillo, Tony Robbins and Brendon Burchard.

So much love for all of you!

Andreea.

References

Dispenza, J. (2014) *You Are the Placebo: Making your mind matter.* Hay House.

Duffield-Thomas, D. (2020) *Chillpreneur: The new rules for creating success, freedom, and abundance on your terms.* Hay House.

Grant, A. (2013) 'Rethinking the Extraverted Sales Ideal: The Ambivert Advantage'. *Psychological Science*, 8/4/2013.

Leahy, R.L. (2006) *The Worry Cure: Stop worrying and start living.* Piatkus.

Rosenthal, R., & Jacobson, L. (1968) *Pygmalion in the Classroom: Teacher expectation and pupils' intellectual development.* Holt, Rinehart & Winston. Revised and expanded 1992.

Sincero, J. (2018) *You Are Badass at Making Money: Master the mindset of wealth.* John Murray Learning.

Wansink, B. and Sobal, J. (2007) 'Mindless Eating: The 200 Daily Food Decisions We Overlook'. *Environment and Behaviour*, Vol 39 Issue 1.